CAPERS IN MY KIRK

What do I believe? How is it that I, a
descendant of dark pagan Celts from the
warm south and of blond Vikings from the
cold north, how is it that I now find myself
professing Christianity and have become an
elder in a respectable Church of Scotland
congregation?

It seems to me that I must first go back to
dark ages in which, as archaeologists surmise,
our ancestors began to understand that there
is more to human existence than the basic
drudgery of finding food and shelter. From
that beginning I ought to find it possible to
make a journey forward to the present time,
tracing as I go the progress of the continuing
battle between the spiritual and material sides
in human nature: a battlefield which is the
world but which can also be found in every
continent, in every country, in every community and in the heart of every man and
woman.

Angus MacVicar

Capers in my Kirk

Confessions of a would-be Christian

ARROW BOOKS

Arrow Books Limited
62—65 Chandos Place, London WC2N 4NW

An imprint of Century Hutchinson Limited

London Melbourne Sydney Auckland
Johannesburg and agencies throughout
the world

First published by Hutchinson 1987
Arrow edition 1988

Printed and bound in Great Britain by
Anchor Brendon Limited, Tiptree, Essex

ISBN 0 09 953450 9

To the Memory of
John R. Gray

Acknowledgements

In writing *Capers in My Kirk* I have made good use of a scholarly book on the subject, *The Church of Scotland* by G.D. Henderson, DD, DLitt., formerly Professor of Church History at the University of Aberdeen.

My grateful thanks are due to Mr R.D. Kernohan, editor of the Church of Scotland magazine, *Life and Work*, whose own book, *Our Church*, has been of help to me.

A.M.

Contents

1
According to John

John was a handsome man, loud and generous. His brushed black hair, patched with grey, camouflaged the toughness, even the roughness of his character.

I knew him well. His main holiday haunt was the parish of Southend at the Mull of Kintyre, where my father laboured as a minister for forty-seven years (1910–57) and in which I have always had my home.

John loved his wife, Sheila, who is a doctor of medicine, and his three sons, Charles, James and David, whose names have a regal Scottish ring. Some years ago Charles and James competed along with their parents in television's *Ask the Family*.

He was elected minister of a congregation whose place of worship is Dunblane Cathedral. In course of time – in 1977 – he became Moderator of the General Assembly of the Church of Scotland and was thus entitled to call himself 'the Very Reverend'.

He was a Tory, true blue and unashamed. He thundered against alcohol, abortion and (at times) the Roman Catholic Church. His moderatorial address to the General Assembly was entitled, characteristically, *Splintering the Gates of Hell*, and its opening words were loud and clear. 'Our society,' he said, 'is sick.'

With deep-set dark eyes alight with power and passion, he went on: 'The sickness manifests itself in all sorts of ways. Inflation is one aspect, for it is a kind of secret theft. Unemployment is another. It is wicked when men and women find it impossible to find work or find it unprofitable to accept work when offered. Alcoholism is another. In Scotland we spent £350,000,000 on alcohol last year, as much as we spent on primary and secondary education combined. Pornography and obscenity are epidemic. As someone has said, Britain badly needs to have its dirty face washed. The increase in the number of abortions is appalling. It is a dreadful reflection that you have much more protection if you are struggling to enter the world as an osprey or an eagle than as a human being.'

At the time Britain had a Labour Government and it was said that such an address had the dubious clang of party politics. I thought it had the genuine clang of Christianity. I am sure John would not have hesitated to say the same salutary words in the year of his death – 1984 – when, under a Tory Government, there was far more unemployment, far more alcoholism, far more pornography and obscenity, far more violence.

He and I followed different party political roads; but he was my friend and friendship always climbs above the petty, self-centred niggling of party politics. And we were in agreement about one thing. The word 'politics' implies 'care for the well being of the people'. It seems that party politics today have a care only for the well being of a party. Religion and politics, therefore, are inextricably mixed, even as they were in the lifetime of Christ and even as they were in the dim ages before Christ's coming, when stone circles and stone idols were the forerunners of churches and chapels, synagogues and temples, mosques and monasteries.

There was a Calvinistic dourness about John which became apparent in his diatribes against alcohol and abortion. And, like my father, he asserted his authority by never appearing in public without his dog-collar – not even while working in his garden. Nevertheless, he was a man who enjoyed life and could shout good-natured abuse at a golf ball which he had struck in a less than skilful way.

Though heavily employed on various church committees, he yet found time to be a conscientious parish minister, rejoicing lustily with wedding guests, sharing the family happiness of a christening and comforting with gentle words the dying and the bereaved.

He had a great care for people, old and young, which in my reckoning is the mark of a good minister. With open honesty he castigated many of them – myself included – for what he regarded as their sins, but he loved them all just the same. And was loved in return.

His sense of humour was rough and ready, like a schoolboy's. Once, as the congregation was skailing (dispersing) after a service in our local church, he stood outside talking to friends and acquaintances in his usual robust manner. I happened to mention that a new doctor was soon to be appointed to the parish, a new doctor who was likely to be female. 'Oh, good!' said John. Then, with a burst of laughter and in a loud voice which startled several douce worshippers almost out of their wits, he remarked: 'Lady doctors are great! I like lady doctors. In fact, I sleep with one!'

His wife shook her head. Her patient, warm smile stifled a few happy expectations of a William Hickey scandal in high and holy places.

For John's moral and physical courage I had constant admiration. Many of his ideas, borrowed from Calvin and John Knox, clashed with the so-called trendiness in modern clerical behaviour. At no time did he allow his clear view of Christianity to be compromised. Some of those views were opposed to mine, especially in regard to drink and the Welfare State; but though he shouted me down in many a rousing argument – and I did my best to retaliate – this again never threatened to cause enmity between us.

His pronouncements at the General Assembly and in the press – and frequently in articles in the Kirk magazine, *Life and Work* – made him unpopular in some quarters, though, significantly, not in his own congregation. Nor in Southend, his holiday hideaway. Muttered criticism, however, did not prevent him from always voicing the truth as he saw it. He believed in God and in the love of God and in the redemption offered by Christ to sinners. This was the source of his courage.

The quality of his courage was tested to the limit when at last a feeling of bodily weakness caused him to consult his doctor. He was told, straightforwardly as he would have wished, that he had cancer and only a few months to live.

He brought the news to Sheila and to his sons. Their courage was tested, too. They faced the imminence of John's death not with a whimper but with defiance. Instead of retiring into sad secrecy they decided that his cancer might be a text for a powerful, continuing sermon: a sermon in action as well as in words.

He told the press of his condition and was interviewed by journalists amazed by his fortitude. With Sheila he appeared on television, and they spoke together of his approaching death calmly and clearly, explaining that their ability to do so lay in the strength of their Christian belief.

To some people this public parade of a private sorrow appeared unseemly. The prim and prissy idea of unseemliness did not occur either to John or to his family. Their purpose, honest and practical, was to demonstrate to readers, viewers and listeners who might be in a similar case that the Christian faith is a powerful source of courage and consolation in the face of death.

One Sunday morning he stood in his pulpit in the cathedral and told his congregation that he was giving up his charge. 'I am not anxious to die,' he said. 'I love life in this glorious world and I love my family and friends. And I might yet be spared a while to write, even if I can no longer preach or speak in public. If, however, I have only a short time to live I shall not complain. I have been spared to preach for forty-five years, and that is a privilege permitted to few.'

Then he went on: 'God has chosen us all for service and salvation. He has chosen us who are here for survival until now, which shows that He has work for us to do, old, young, active or retired. A man is immortal until his work is done.'

That sermon was preached in February 1984. Six months later he was dead. I believe that in the last year of his life he had done as much for the cause of Christianity as he had done in his whole previous ministry.

A few weeks before he died he wrote to me:

'*Bees in My Bonnet* is the best yet. But you have still the last chapter to write. Tell us what your convictions are now about Man and God, about this life and the meaning of it all. It *can't* be just golf! Some thoughts lie too deep for tears or words, but let us have some words which come to the surface as the past seventy years fly past.'

I told John I would try. I did not tell him that such a task

presented almost insuperable difficulties, especially to a confused, blundering, uncertain individual like myself. I did not
tell him either that while I have always wanted to be a
Christian I have not always lived like one and that at times my
faith has teetered on the brink of a great chasm of disbelief.

Responding to his challenge, however, I will try to write
down the 'words' he wanted, though they may not be quite the
ones he expected. Like Frank Sinatra, I must 'do it my way'.

What do I believe? How is it that I, a descendant of dark
pagan Celts from the warm south and of blond Vikings from
the cold north, how is it that I now find myself professing
Christianity and have become an elder in a respectable Church
of Scotland congregation?

It seems to me that I must first go back to dark ages in which,
as archaeologists surmise, our ancestors began to understand
that there is more to human existence than the basic drudgery
of finding food and shelter. From that beginning I ought to
find it possible to make a journey forward to the present time,
tracing as I go the progress of the continuing battle between
the spiritual and material sides in human nature: a battlefield
which is the world but which can also be found in every
continent, in every country, in every community and in the
heart of every man and woman.

I propose to make this journey within and around the
marches of the parish of Southend at the Mull of Kintyre –
where St Columba is said to have first set foot, literally as well
as figuratively, in the land now called Scotland – because in
Southend, in microcosm, there exists the whole sacred and
secular history of Scotland and the Church of Scotland.

(Southend is not unique in this. Hundreds of parishes in
Scotland, urban and rural, contain the same historical clues.
But Southend is my nursemaid and my love. I know it and its
people and understand them best.)

During the journey I hope to discover guide-posts. These
will take the shape of ancient stones and ancient manuscripts,
of legends and histories concerning the inhabitants, of more
modern books and of my own contacts with people in a
kirk-centred community.

All this may mean, as I struggle to find the 'words', the
cancellation of many a good game of golf. A discipline which

would have commended itself to the Very Reverend John R. Gray, VRD, DD, MA, BD, ThM.

2
Lay Stone on Stone

The peninsula of Kintyre, from the Gaelic *Ceann Tire*, 'head of the land', is like a sturdy leg upholding the body of Scotland. One of its favourite sons, the Rev. A. Wylie Blue, has remarked that 'without Kintyre, Scotland wouldn't have a leg to stand on'. His joke has more substance than may appear on the surface.

If Kintyre is the leg, then the parish of Southend, which includes the Mull at its southern extremity, can be described as the foot. The Norsemen, adapting from the Gaelic *Sail Tire*, called it *Saltiri*, 'the heel of the land'.

It can also be described as a pierhead for pilgrims and adventurers moving to and from Ireland, who, throughout the centuries, have faced and crossed the narrow, uneasy waters of the North Channel: *Struithe na Maoile* as the Gaelic writers call it. The distance between the lighthouse at the Mull of Kintyre and Fair Head in Antrim is less than twelve miles. From where I sit at my window I can see the Irish hills, grey rounded lumps above the white-flecked sea. They are only seventeen miles away.

It is said that the population of Southend is one-third Highland, one-third Lowland and one-third Irish. There is truth in this, just as there is truth in what somebody else has said of us: 'Though they profess to be Presbyterians, the folk of Southend are really one-third Protestant, one-third Roman Catholic and one-third pagan.' But there are many more people in Scotland of whom the same can be said, including supporters of Rangers and Celtic.

Southend has an area of about fifty square miles. It consists of two comparatively flat valleys, those of the River Breckrie and the River Con. They are separated by a ridge of low hills running southward. On the east they are guarded by red sandstone cliffs and high stretches of tussocky moorland, on the west by mountainous country coloured purple by heather. Up there, high in the peat-scented air, buzzards and eagles fly.

The atmosphere in Southend is clean and fresh, because the prevailing wind blows in from the open Atlantic. There are no problems of pollution, though some fastidious noses may be turned away when dung is spread on stubble, and silage is decanted on green land as food for hungry cattle.

Sometimes farmers and gardeners reckon the air is a little too fresh when gales shrivel the potato shaws and rip slates and corrugated iron from the rooftops. In our bungalow by the sea my wife, Jean, calls the wind evil names when it whips up the spray and sullies her shining windows. Compared with the east coast of Scotland, however, the climate of Southend is generally mild, which may be due to the influence of the Gulf Stream.

The people of the parish live in the farms and farm-cottages in the valleys and in the village which is separated only by a narrow strip of golf course from the mouth of the Con.

The village is made up of a long row of buildings along one side of the main road. An inn, a hall, a doctor's surgery, a shop and a post office stand shoulder to shoulder with houses council and private. Among the slate roofs television aerials sprout like weeds, most of them pointing towards Belfast across the North Channel. On the other side of the road, in dignified isolation among arable fields, looms a house that was once a manse, flanked by a garage that was once a church. They belonged to the United Free Church, now happily merged with the Church of Scotland. Donnie McKerral, Jean's nephew, uses them as the headquarters of his road-haulage business.

Half a mile southward, fronting black coastal rocks, are more private houses (including ours, which is called Achna-mara, from the Gaelic, meaning 'Seafield'), a hotel, a graveyard surrounding a ruined thirteenth-century church and, on a knoll above the graveyard, a flat rock in which is incised a footprint: a footprint more than 2000 years old.

Half a mile north, in the valley of the Con, the church and

manse of St Blaan stand with open doors, serving the spiritual needs of the people. Around the manse are sheltered trees, a comparatively rare phenomenon in this windswept parish. No trees shelter the bare, grey kirk. Unmuffled, its bell rings out for Sunday worship: a bell with a crack in it; a bell salvaged many years ago from a sailing ship wrecked on Sanda, a small island lying two miles off the south-east shore.

The 'Kirk at the Corner' was built in 1773 and opened for public worship in February 1774. Americans, Canadians, Australians and New Zealanders come regularly to sit in the varnished pews of Norwegian pine: the very pews in which their ancestors sat before they sailed away, in sadness, from the pier at Dunaverty, forced to emigrate, as the records show, because of 'poverty and lack of work'.

One day in summer I took Mrs Harvey B. Hunter of Charlotte, North Carolina, to the farm in Southend where her ancestor, James Caldwell, was born. I took her also to the 'Kirk at the Corner' in which he had worshipped in the hard days before he emigrated, in August 1774, to begin a new and more prosperous life in America. I showed her the pew, unchanged in 200 years, which had been used by the Caldwell family. The old lady sat where her forebears had sat. Tears came into her eyes. 'Oh my,' she said in her lovely accent, 'this is the most wunnerful day of ma life!'

Near the church are the primary school and the school-houses (one old, one new). They are flanked by a playground where, as children, we played rounders with a Sorbo ball and a bat made from a branch of willow or an old broom handle. Guarding the playground from the road is a high stone wall, over which only the most daring boys used to drop, encouraged by the shrieks of admiring little girls. The only time I dropped I sprained my ankle. The little girls laughed. One of them was called Jean McKerral. She has been my wife now for fifty years and is still inclined to laugh when I make a fool of myself. A frequent occurrence. Unfortunately the sprain was not considered severe enough to keep me off school for an afternoon.

The population of Southend hovers around 500 and has done so since 1910 when my father was inducted minister of the parish. It includes mainly farmers and farmworkers; but there are also many who commute daily to Campbeltown, ten miles away, to work in offices, shops, garages and computer centres. In some of the little houses strewn like bright pebbles along the valleys live people who have retired to the peace of a community with only one main road running into it and in which neighbourly interest is so strong that pretentious behaviour tends to die like moss among healthy grass. In which, too, almost everybody is a member of or has connections with the Church, the WRI, the golf club, the drama club, the badminton club, the soccer and rugby clubs, and the indoor sports club which thrives in winter in one of the church halls.

We are lucky. Because of our geographical location, fairly remote from urban influence, we can still exist as a viable community. We have our own minister and our own doctor, which means that our souls and bodies are tended in an individual and warmly human way and not on the basis of impersonal numbers on the cards of a team ministry or group practice.

Through television, radio, newspapers and books we are always kept well informed about national and international affairs and can therefore, perhaps, view them more objectively than some who struggle in their midst. When I am able to afford the air fare I can breakfast in Southend and lunch in London. There are many more communities of this kind in Scotland, England, Ireland and Wales, a fact which blinkered bureaucrats often seem to forget.

The first known inhabitants of Southend (and, indeed, of Scotland) lived in the Mesolithic period (*c.*6000–3000 BC). Discoveries of their distinctively worked flint and quartz implements on several recently excavated building sites in Campbeltown would seem to indicate that the Mesolithic people moved about in small groups as hunters and fishermen.

At one of these sites over a thousand waste flakes of flint, along with hide-scraping implements and a chisel-headed tool, were found on a twenty-five-foot raised beach. A number of the flints were water-worn. Archaeologists deduce from this that their owners must have occupied the foreshore when, after the Ice Age, the sea was beginning to recede to its present shoreline.

Not long ago, on the island of Rhum in the Hebrides, a ploughman uncovered a hoard of bloodstone flakes. Archaeologist Caroline Whickham-Jones immediately recognized their significance and excavations were carried out. Among the flakes were found stone axes, hammer-heads, carbonized hazelnut shells and other debris which made her suspect that here was the location of a Mesolithic family factory which made weapons and other artefacts not only for themselves but also for communities in other areas.

Perhaps the most interesting discovery was a core of bloodstone from which had been struck a number of sharp blades. Two of the blades lay beside it. They fitted together. They also fitted perfectly into the core.

What kind of machine-tools did the Mesolithic manufacturers use? Hammers and punches made from reindeer antlers? Whatever they were, Mesolithic technology was obviously in a more advanced state than has sometimes been supposed.

Nor were the people themselves the rude, slope-headed, knuckle-dragging savages, conversing in grunts, portrayed in some boys' magazines. They may have worn clothes made from skins; but then, so do many fur-coated, expensively shod ladies and gentlemen in the present era. They may have lived in tents or huts made from hides; but then, many of us today live in jerry-built houses of match-stick construction which can scarcely be called fully wind and water proof. They may have been shorter in stature than modern Scots – and more weather-beaten – but in all other aspects I think they would look very much like us, with a developed language and, again like us, an ability to use their environment.

What is now certain is that they possessed a sense of family and community and approved the idea – wherever it came from – that to help their neighbours by supplying them with tools for living was a good thing: a factor in the attainment of their own well being.

Did they worship anything or anybody? There is, as yet, no telling, though it would seem, from a study of the exquisite cave-paintings of animals at Altamira in Spain and in other parts of Europe, dated even earlier than the Mesolithic Age, that the minds of people who lived perhaps 10,000 years ago were frequently occupied by thoughts which had little relevance to a crude struggle for survival.

Using boats made of wood and hide, the Mesolithic family in Rhum may have moved there from the south, perhaps from Kintyre or even Southend.

Throughout the Mesolithic period the Ice Age in Scotland gradually came to an end, accompanied by an improvement in temperature and climate. Rich growth stirred in the ground. In the fifth millennium BC the Mesolithic fishermen began to find strangers in their midst: Neolithic farmers venturing into new fertile territory from southern parts. Such parts included Ireland, so close to the Mull of Kintyre across the narrow sea. Their stone axes, arrow heads and chambered cairns have been found in Southend, in other parts of Kintyre and throughout the whole of Scotland.

From the Aros Moss, over the mountain-tops from Southend and between Campbeltown and Machrihanish, peat samples have been taken. Upon analysis these show clearly that towards the end of the Mesolithic period there was a marked decline in elm pollen and a corresponding increase in grass and weed pollen. (Among the weeds ribwort plantain, with its bountiful seed spikes, seems to have been most common. To this day ribwort plantain is a source of nourishment for birds. Was it once a source of nourishment for humans?)

It can be deduced, therefore, that during this period the Neolithic farmers were busily employed in cutting down trees with their stone axes and, in the reclaimed ground, encouraging the growth of vegetation suitable for human and animal consumption.

There is no record of how the Mesolithic people got on with their new neighbours. But I have a picture in my mind of the douce, industrious Neolithic farmers being somewhat upset by the aristocratic Mesolithic hunters rampaging blithely through their growing crops in pursuit of elk, wild boar or reindeer.

On the lower reaches of the Breckrie valley in Southend there can be found small, tough trees which trace their descent from the ancient Caledonian forests. High above the valley, among the silent hills and not far from the bog source of the Con, are the remains of a Neolithic settlement as old as the trees. The twin pillars which mark the entrance to a chambered cairn at its centre were in position long before Egyptian slaves built the pyramid of Cheops and the Sphinx.

In their matter-of-fact, scientific way archaeologists list the cairn as Lochorodale 2 (ARG32). They continue: 'Severely disturbed by stone-robbing, it appears as a grass-grown stony mound of irregular outline, measuring 23 metres in length and 15 metres in greatest breadth and standing up to 1.2 metres in height, with the longer axis aligned almost East and West . . . The chamber, which is aligned approximately East and West measures about 4.3 metres in length by up to 1.2 metres in width internally.'

Far below is the farmhouse of Lochorodale, where often, as a boy, during a clipping, I used to help catch the sheep and bring them to the shearers on their stools. Where, too, after a sumptuous supper of broth and stewed mutton, I used to sit with the shepherds and listen to their stories, humorous, ribald, tragic, ghostly.

Behind the chambered cairn is a rocky eminence on which I can now stand and wonder and imagine things – and remember one particular story told by one particular shepherd.

There to the west and north and east are the turf-covered remains of a wall which once contained the settlement. To the south is a deep gorge down which chatters the infant Con. A hill road breaks into the wall from the west, runs through it past the cairn and breaks out of it again to the east. No doubt, over the centuries, the wall was rebuilt and repaired many times. It may still have been useful to cattle-rearing crofters less than two hundred years ago.

But I can believe that the first wall was built by the Neolithic people who later, around 3000 BC, also built the first cairn. Within its bounds lie scattered many weathered stones which look as if they have been shaped by tools.

There is a bubbling spring of fresh water in the north-east corner and a little stream plunging away from it, down into the Con. The high rocks through which the stream runs as it enters the river are covered with ivy. This interests me, because the presence of ivy is often a sign that at one time gardeners lived nearby.

Less than two miles away another Neolithic chambered

cairn, Lochorodale 1, is situated beside a depression, now drained and dry, which was once, in historic times, a small loch. There is a stone there, too, with ivy growing on it.

Near the spring at Lochorodale 2 is an area of bright green turf. When you stand on it and flex your knees and push with your feet the turf heaves up and down like a constipated trampoline. From beneath it there emerges a sucking, gurgling sound, which indicates that it covers a considerable volume of water.

In Kintyre we call such a thing a wallee, a word which may be derived from 'wall-spring', meaning water trapped between stratified rocks. As children we were warned never to go near such places in case our feet broke through the turf and we were engulfed like the villain in *The Hound of the Baskervilles*. There was a wallee on the farm of Kilblaan near the manse; and of course, as boys, my brothers and I danced on it many times, thrilled by the act of rebellion and by the hint of danger.

Could it be that the wallee in the vicinity of Lochorodale 2 conceals a structured pool, where 5000 years ago Neolithic people bathed and washed their garments?

This is only one of the many questions I wish could be answered about Lochorodale 2, lonely and deserted among the hills. But it is a listed site and an amateur archaeologist like myself is forbidden by royal decree to dig in it or even to turn a stone. But at least I can dig into my imagination and turn the stones of memory.

That numbers of people once lived and worked here is certain. Standing above the cairn I know it to be true. I recollect the story told by old Archie Campbell as we relaxed in the big kitchen in Lochorodale farmhouse after a clipping, with the aroma of good whisky in the air.

The light of a paraffin lamp shone on his high, bald forehead. White whiskers did not conceal a twinkle in his eyes or the humorous set of his full-lipped mouth.

He had been in Campbeltown at a sheep sale, he told me, and was walking home across the hills in the midnight dark. The stars were out, but there was no moon. As he climbed the steep brae which rises from Lochorodale farmhouse to the ancient site he began to feel uneasy. There was silence everywhere: no bird or animal sounds, usually common at night, not even a tinkling from the water of the Con.

He followed the track as it led through the crumbling turf of the south-east wall. Looming up on his left he saw the tall stones of the cairn, apparently huger than usual in the dim light. He thought he saw movement among them but still heard no sound.

He tried to hurry on. His feet seemed to drag. It was as if he were being hemmed in by unseen creatures. The coldness of fear stiffened the back of his neck.

Again he thought he saw movement, this time close by on his right. But when he raised his crook and struck out in that direction the stick touched nothing.

He was a young man then, fit and strong as a shepherd should be. He began to run, out through the west wall and on to the brae which led down to Dalsmirren, where he lived.

Then he stopped, panting and sweating. He listened. He heard the small sounds which had been absent before. The sweat on his body grew cold. He began to shake a little, but he was no longer afraid.

'Had you a dram in you, Archie?' asked one of his friends, winking at me.

'Well, only a very wee one,' he said. 'But I put a good few inside me when I got to Dalmirren!'

I have never been to Lochorodale 2 in the dark, but even in the daylight, as I stand now above the cairn – stone cold sober – I can well understand how he felt. There is strangeness here.

> A savage place! as holy and enchanted
> As e'er beneath a waning moon was haunted . . .

What was the purpose of the cairn?

Digs at other Neolithic sites in the country have revealed that such cairns contained communal tombs. With the bodies were buried pottery vessels, including round-bottomed, hand-made bowls and cups, some lugged, some plain. As the number of tombs increased and the cairns were enlarged, the original undecorated bowls and cups were replaced by larger and more elaborate vessels decorated by channelling, incision and stabbing with some kind of sharp tool and, more rarely, by impressed cord.

Originally, therefore, the cairns may have been built as

'churches', meeting places for members of a large family group. When they died people were buried near the 'church' and, in the case of important individuals, within its structure. Westminster Abbey contains many tombs. At Keil, in Southend, the ruined thirteenth-century church of St Colomba is surrounded by the parish cemetery, while inside it are the graves of abbots, knights and lairds, some dating back many centuries. (The walls of St Columba's are covered with ivy. Only a few yards away is St Columba's Well. To the hillside rocks above it cling masses of ivy.)

But were those ancient Neolithic buildings used as 'churches' in the way that we use churches? Did people congregate in and around them in order to worship someone – or something? Nobody knows. But it is a fact that all of them are built facing east, as are the great majority of church buildings all over the world. The sun rises in the east.

Did the Neolithic farmers have priests or ministers to conduct burial services and to preach a gospel? Nobody knows that, either. But their ancestors had travelled far, encountering the enmity of other human tribes, the savage attacks of wild beasts and the harshness of new environments. Now, in order to protect themselves, they had gathered in communities, because in some minds an idea must have been burgeoning: the idea that men and women, for the sake of their own and their neighbours' well being, should love one another and so live in peace together.

Such a concept, however, had to be presented to the people and its logical consequences explained to them. By whom? Might not this have been a time when religious leaders emerged to bring spiritual and social succour to anxious people sorely in need of it?

That the Neolithic people eventually achieved a considerable degree of sophistication is apparent in numerous Neolithic remains in this country – notably at Stonehenge in Wiltshire and Callanish on the island of Lewis in the Hebrides – all of which are of a much later date than Lochorodale 2 and other even cruder monuments in Kintyre. According to the archaeologists Stonehenge and Callanish could only have been designed by individuals well versed in astronomy and advanced building techniques and erected, in practical terms, by enormous gangs of manual labourers. How otherwise could such huge stones, some weighing as much as twenty-five tons, have been quarried, shaped, transported and finally planted firmly in positions which relate to various stars, including, of course, the sun?

Such evidence would seem to indicate the development of a society not unlike that of Egypt at the time: a ruling class of priestly scholars and a subservient class of workers. No doubt the priestly scholars – as in Egypt – began with good intentions, preaching not only the benefits of love and peace but also the benefits of astronomy in their seasonal planning of agricultural projects. Like certain modern 'religious' leaders – and like all public relations officers today – they buttressed their arguments by making good use of the superstitious element in human nature. They represented gods as fearful beings, threatening terrible punishments for those who disobeyed their commands. And in the end, intoxicated by their own increasing moral and material power, they came to believe that they themselves were gods.

The moral factor in their rule diminished. The material factor became all important. In order to maintain their worldly eminence they made slaves of their workers. They were even prepared to kill those who might question their 'religious' beliefs, camouflaging their real intent by calling such victims sacrifices to the gods.

The true meaning of love and peace were forgotten, 'evanishing amid the storm'. The only love allowed was the love of Big Brother, the only peace that of the most powerful weapons available.

I am only imagining that this is what happened. There is no documentary or firm archaeological evidence to support such a scenario, and it is probable that none will ever be found. But similar developments have occurred – are still occurring – in historic times. Why should they not in prehistoric times? We are all 'Jock Tamson's bairns'.

And folk memories are unconscionably long a-dying.

My father (the Padre) was a native of North Uist. When eleven years old I went with him there on holiday. One Sunday morning, as we walked along the road skirting the seaweed-scented white strand at Claddach Kirkibost, we met an old woman, stooped a little and wearing a worsted shawl. She spoke in the Gaelic (which was the Padre's native tongue), and we exchanged greetings.

Then she put her hand, wrinkled and brown, on my father's sleeve. 'Are you going to the stones?' she asked him, almost in a whisper.

'Yes, we are.'

We moved on. 'What on earth did she mean – going to the stones?' I said.

He had a curious, distant look. 'It's a Gaelic old-word,' he told me. 'Where it comes from I'm not quite sure. She meant, Are you going to the church?'

3
Barbarian Prophets

In archaeological terms the Neolithic Age (*c.* 3000–2000 BC) was followed by the Bronze Age (*c.*2000–500 BC). But in the blurred, overlapping centuries changes in the spiritual and social climate were taking place.

In Southend and Kintyre, as elsewhere, the imposing, collective tombs of the Neolithic people were progressively replaced by individual cists and graves, sometimes found under round cairns or barrows. The building of great stone 'churches' as meeting places – and possibly, burial places – appears to have gone out of fashion. Instead it is reasonably certain that the Bronze Age descendants of the original Neolithic farmers congregated for 'religious' purposes in secluded groves – or hutments of wood and turf – close to the sites of their swelling graveyards.

Reasons for the change may be found not only in the new attitude towards godliness but also in economic factors. In modern times similar factors can be seen at work. Slave labour is now regarded by the majority as an evil. Towering 'cathedrals' are giving place to humbler – and cheaper – shrines.

My wife, Jean, is the descendant of a family of McKerrals. In the eighteenth century they lived at the shore-mouth of a lonely glen through which runs a stream marking the northeast boundary of Southend parish. They were crofters and fishermen.

The McKerrals' house was typical of the period in Scotland, walled with clay-girt stones and roofed with heather thatch. The living room, bedroom, byre and other outhouses were built in a continuous long line. It is probable that like the 'black houses' of my father's youth in North Uist smoke from the peat fire in the living room escaped through a hole in the roof. In the winter the bedroom would be warmed by the body heat of cattle – and sometimes pigs – on the other side of a partition wall which did not quite reach the rafters. Their food would consist mainly of fish, oatmeal, potatoes and kale. And occasionally, when a beast died, of beef or pork. The women-folk of the time were expert spinners and weavers. Most of the McKerral clothes would be home-made.

The site is called Balnabraid. On a bleak, bare winter's afternoon the ruins of the house can still be seen, though in summer they are difficult to locate among the green growth of saplings, bracken and grass.

Jean's brothers, Archie and Davie, emigrated to Southern Rhodesia before World War II and farmed there for many years. Once, when both were on holiday in Scotland, they visited Balnabraid, cut a piece of turf from what had once been their ancestors' garden and took it away with them. Archie and Davie are now dead, but that piece of turf is still part of the lawn of a Zimbabwean farm.

Between the ruins of Balnabraid and the seashore, on a twenty-five-foot raised beach platform of land overlooking the stream, there is a cairn which provides some evidence of the changes which occurred in the overlapping period between the Neolithic and Bronze Ages. It startles me to realize that Balnabraid's community was a flourishing one when Homer wrote his celebrated scripts featuring Helen of Troy.

The original cairn may have been Neolithic, but over the centuries – between 2000 BC and 500 BC – it was completely submerged by numerous burial cists, some on top of others. A few contained food vessels, tools and weapons of widely differing dates. For example, a beaker found in one deep-laid cist on a slightly higher level is said to belong to the fifteenth or fourteenth century BC. A bronze razor of a type now thought to date back only to 1000 BC has been discovered on a higher level still.

What does such evidence suggests? Did the Bronze Age people come to believe – as many people believe today – that the inborn human desire for love and peace cannot be achieved in a Big Brother context? As a result, did they try to achieve it in the context of a freer family and community life? Did their concept of a God change as well as their attitudes to 'religious' observances?

These are questions which cannot be answered with any authority. But, groping in the dark, I have a feeling that something like this happened over the dim-lit centuries during which the great stone cairns were replaced by ones of a more homely character.

But even in a society based on family and community life leaders naturally arise to show anxious people how they may accomplish their instinctive desire for love and peace and to formulate laws which they believe will be of help in the process. Forced to concentrate most of their thought and energy upon making a living for themselves and their families, and thus finding little time or inclination to think out problems of existence for themselves, the people allow their leaders to garner more and more moral and secular power. Soon the wheel of 'religious' life grinds round full circle. Instead of to Big Brother, they find themselves in thrall to a number of Wee Brothers. If we admit – as we must – that fascism and communism are 'religions', then we are seeing it all happening again today, throughout the world.

The 'religious' leaders who became powerful in the late Bronze Age (as it merged with the Iron Age) appear to have been the Druids.

The real Druids can be apprehended only vaguely even after exhaustive research by archaeologists and prehistorians. As if through a swirling fog we may catch a glimpse of them as 'barbarian prophets and prognosticators' who attended ceremonies (the sacrifices being both animal and human), read omens and practised magic. Such shadowy figures bear no resemblance to the white-robed romantics who raise their arms to the sun as it first appears above Stonehenge's heel-stone on a Midsummer's Day.

Druids are mentioned by Posidonius, Strabo, Pliny, Caesar and other classical writers, but it is difficult to perceive their true character from references which are often contradictory.

Pomponius Nola calls them 'professors' of wisdom. They are often described (notably by Caesar) as 'the most just of men' who wielded considerable judicial power. Posidonius emphasizes their authority in civil and criminal cases as well as in questions of property and boundaries.

On the other hand, Strabo tells of how they made human sacrifices by stabbing captives in the back. He also describes a horrific Druid rite, in which human and animal victims were first wounded by arrows – or impaled on sharpened stakes – then thrown, some of them still alive, into a huge wickerwork figure (*kolosson*) which was finally set on fire.

Pliny makes reference to yet another rite practised by Druids. This took place when mistletoe was found growing on an oak tree, an occurrence rare enough to suggest to them that it had been put there specially by divine intention.

The time chosen was the sixth day of the moon. Preparations for a feast were made and two white bulls procured for sacrifice. A white-robed Druid climbed the tree and cut a branch from the mistletoe with a golden sickle, allowing it to fall on a white cloak. Then the two bulls were killed and placed upon an altar. (Could a sickle made of pure, softish gold have cut through a tough mistletoe branch? I doubt it. Might not the blade have been of polished, sharpened bronze which shone like gold?)

Outside Keil churchyard in Southend there is a small cave known locally as the Druid's Cave. Inside it there is an oblong slab, approximately one and a half metres by one metre, constructed from the bedrock of the cliff above. The earth has now silted up around it, but two or three thousand years ago it may have stood about one and a half metres high. On its flat surface are two depressions, deep and smooth. My guru in archaeology, Dr Martin Munro, suggests that originally these were ordinary cup-marks but that at a later date they were used as 'bait mortars' in which shellfish were broken up to supply fishermen's hooks. Such fishermen were probably the Iron Age inhabitants of a much larger cave nearby, relics of whose occupation are now on view in the museum at Campbeltown.

What was the purpose of those original 'ordinary cup-marks', which appear on slabs of stone in Southend, in Scotland, in Europe and in many other parts of the world? Archaeologists and prehistorians, lacking any kind of positive evidence, are unable to answer the question. Could it be that at first they were made to receive and contain blood from the sacrifices? When sacrifices became outmoded, were cup-marks then incised in stones as 'religious' symbols in much the same way as 'the blood of the Lamb' is depicted today on stained-glass windows?

What is the human story which lies behind the rise and fall of the Druids? As people found that their instinctive yearning for love and peace could not be satisfied by the Big Brothers of the Neolithic Age, did they now find that it could not be satisfied either by the Druidic Wee Brothers?

I think that in both cases priestly scholars emerged in communities to preach high ideals. The well being of the people was their priority. But as time passed and the people, glad as always to shirk the issue and delegate moral responsi-bility, were willing to grant them more and more power, their care for others was translated into care for themselves. Un-happy people, perceiving dimly what was happening, made efforts to assert themselves. The priestly scholars decided that the only way in which they could maintain their power was by force: force both psychological and physical. Ancient 'gods' were resurrected to punish what they themselves chose to define as 'sins'. 'Sacrifices' had to be made in order to subdue rebellion in thought and action. A rule of love became a rule of fear, echoes of which remain with us to this day: 'The fear of the Lord is the beginning of wisdom.'

But the spirit of man never becomes completely subservient. There is always a time when the dams of repression and false propaganda burst their walls, first in a trickle, then in an increasing flood. This is what may have happened in the Neolithic Age when the tall, overbearing megalithic monu-ments were replaced by more modest cairns, and again in the Bronze Age, when the power of the Druids dwindled with the advent of the Iron Age (*c.*500 BC – *c.*AD 400).

In the Iron Age yet another dam burst, in spectacular fashion. Christ was born.

A prominent hill in the parish of Southend is Tapoc. I can only guess at the derivation of the name. But 'tap' is Scots for 'top' and 'ock' is a Scots diminutive. Perhaps, therefore, it simply means 'Wee Top'. This describes Tapoc well enough when it is compared with the Big Tops among the mountains at the Mull.

It climbs gently to about 700 feet and overlooks the village like a benign aunt. Indeed, Tapoc's eastern slope is shaped like a reclining Victorian matron with a high bosom and long, spreading skirt. The Sleeping Lady keeps one sharp eye, in the shape of a clump of yellow-flowered whins, turned towards the village.

(Within recent years another clump of whins has appeared on the silhouette. It gives our Sleeping Lady the semblance of a moustache. I have implored my friend Colonel Hamish Taylor who, with his son Donald, owns the ground on which she lies, to give her a shave. He says he will do it when his constant struggle with Common Market agricultural regulations gives him time.)

I stand on Tapoc's top (which, according to our local geologist, Dr Ian Munro, is part of the rim of an extinct volcano) and survey the two valleys sweeping down, green and fertile, to the sea. But in past ages these valleys were not fertile. They consisted of boggy marshland, with the sea running into the many shouldered hollows now under cultivation. On the farm of Low Machrimore (which includes the Sleeping Lady), in a field about half a mile from the mouth of the Con, there are a number of stone slabs. They project from the topmost turf to an escarpment overlooking a grassy hollow. This hollow once contained an arm of the sea. It is possible, therefore, that some of the slabs are the remains of an ancient pier or jetty.

And because the valleys were damp and dangerous, the early inhabitants of this inhospitable country congregated on the high ground where they could scratch out a livelihood among the rocks. Along the central ridge, not far from where I stand on Tapoc, I can see beyond the skirts of the Sleeping Lady the faint, grass and whin-grown outline of a fortified hilltop settlement known as Cnoch Araich. It existed in the Iron Age, more than 2000 years ago, and probably even before that.

Cnoc Araich covers six and a quarter acres of rough ground, some of it now cultivated by Archie Cameron, the present owner of High Machrimore. Its defences consist of triple ramparts of heaped earth and stones cast out of double ditches. Archaeologists suggest that this was once the headquarters of the *Epidii*, the Celtic tribe which prompted the Greek map-maker Ptolemy, in the second century AD, to call Kintyre *Epidion Akron*, 'the promontory of the horse-people'.

The Irish Gaels called Southend *Aird Echdi i Cinn Tire*, 'the headland of the Echde in Kintyre', Echde meaning 'the tribe with the horse as its totem'. In Kintyre there are still many people called McEachran, from the Gaelic, 'sons of the horse-men'. (As Barbara, my wife's old daily help used to say, 'It mak's ye wunner!')

It is easy to imgine Cnoc Araich as the centre of a community. A busy little village, with the farmers and their herd boys moving out in the mornings to the lower ground to 'plough and sow, to reap and mow' and to guide grazing cattle away from the treacherous marshland; and in the evenings returning within the defences again, carrying their crude implements and driving in their beasts for milking and rest.

Inside the walls of rubble and turf must not they feel safer, because outside is the darkness, full of prowling wild animals and evil spirits? In beehive houses of timber and thatch, after eating, they sit around their peat and wood fires, singing songs about ancient heroes and also, inevitably, about their neighbours. And as the little clay bowls of corn spirit are passed around in a glow of well being, do they not become philosophical and discuss together the sources of their good fortune in being at peace? There is greed and suspicion and conflict and hate. But there is also friendship and love and the solace of being together. Who or what, they may be asking themselves, is the divine spirit which indicates to them the way to happiness – a spirit hard to find in a 'religion' dominated by cruel 'gods' and evil spirits?

They have been taught in past centuries that in order to achieve 'holiness' they must obey the Druids and, on occasions, make sacrifices. Their daily work must be done in accordance with certain rules: for example, the building of a house or a peat-stack has always to proceed from left to right. Building in the contrary direction, from right to left, would be playing into the hands of the Evil One. Our ancestors had a word for 'right to left'. They called it 'widdershins'.

I suppose this rule originated in dim and distant ages when

people worshipped the sun. The punishments for disobedience must have been severe and terrible, because even when the sun ceased to be a principal object of worship people continued, by inbred fear, to follow it. Bricklayers still lay bricks from left to right. Farmers at harvest time, when they used to make corn-stacks, built them round from left to right. I dig my garden from left to right, and ever since I was a boy in a Christian manse I have put my left sock on first. And my left shoe also. Were I, in a moment of sleepy forgetfulness, to do the opposite I should live for the rest of the day in fear of imminent disaster.

I remember a day when I sat in the clubhouse, putting on my golf shoes before competing with my friend Duncan Watson II in a Monthly Medal Final. In a moment of suppressed excitement I forgot my habit and put on the right one first, a fact which I realized only when taking up my stance on the first tee. Spirit thoroughly undermined, I lost that match – 'out in the country', as golfers say when they are reluctant to announce cold numbers like 8 and 7. Which may serve as an illustration of the psychological power exercised by the prehistoric Big and Wee Brothers.

But in the Iron Age, as shepherds watched their flocks near Bethlehem and herd boys watched their cattle in Kintyre, the inhabitants of Cnoc Araich, like their contemporaries in other parts of Scotland, were beginning to doubt the wisdom of the Druids. Sacrificial practices, belief in evil spirits – even the rule of left to right – all made for uncomfortable living. Constant fear is rocky ground in which to cultivate peace. Love is much more fertile, as they were able to prove, comfortable within the defences of Cnoc Araich and within the fellowship of a community.

But who – or what – must they worship in order to achieve such a blessing? The sun? The sun gave them warmth and growth. It raised their spirits when it shone down in splendour. But sometimes it deserted them, and the weather grew cold and dark under looming clouds. The Epidii were looking for another kind of 'god' – a constant god who could uphold their spirits even when the lightning flashed and the thunder rolled. They longed to be free of fear and comforted by love.

Then Christ came to the Middle East. His message spread

westward. Pagan people, such as the Epidii in Kintyre, were ready to listen, because in such a message they glimpsed freedom: freedom not only physical but spiritual as well.

4
One-legged on a Pillar

Roman rule provided peace, order and unity. It also provided
good roads along which merchants and missionaries could
travel in comparative safety. These were circumstances which
encouraged the spread of Christ's gospel throughout Europe.
And, later, in Britain.

When Christianity came to Britain is uncertain; but in AD
200 Tertullian was reporting that there were 'haunts of the
Britons, inaccessible to the Romans, but subjugated to Christ'.
I imagine it came, carried and exemplified not by great missionary apostles but by ordinary folk going about their daily
business, like the slave nursemaid who is said to have persuaded Monica, the mother of St Augustine, to become a
Christian. The anti-Christian Celsus was perturbed to discover that Christianity was being practised by 'workers in
wool and leather and fullers and persons of the most unin-
structed and rustic character'.

Then, in 313, the Emperor Constantine became a Christian
and declared Christianity legal. With the exception of Julian
(361–3) all his successors were professing Christians; and
eventually the Emperor Theodosius made Christianity the
official religion of the Roman Empire.

From small and simple beginnings the Church was now
organized and strong, enjoying powerful leadership. Theology
became a popular study. Dignified liturgies and forms of
service were devised and bishops, presbyters and deacons
(priestly scholars) appointed to oversee the work of the ordinary clergy. Great preachers emerged, such as Chrystostom,
whose byname was 'Golden Mouth'.

The trouble about organization, the trouble about power
jealously wielded by a few is that individual freedom of

thought tends to be hampered and even, at times, crushed altogether. It probably happened in the Neolithic Age and again in the Bronze Age and Iron Age. Now it was happening in the Christian era, in the Church itself.

After Constantine's grant of toleration Christianity grew respectable, even fashionable. Lip service to the faith was given by some people who saw it as a means to increase their social and material status. (Robert Burns had a phrase for them, the 'unco guid'.) But there were Christians who believed that such hypocrisy threatened to secularize and corrupt the Church. In a bid to save their own souls they drew apart from ordinary Church life. They invented monasticism.

St Anthony is thought to have been the founder of Christian monasticism. (The idea burgeoned in other religions, too, particularly in Buddhism.) He was an Egyptian, born about 250 AD. In the Bible he read the story told by Matthew of the rich young ruler and was impelled to give away all his possessions and endure an ascetic life in his native village. But even this did not satisfy his desire to distance himself from churchiness. Finally he took himself off into the desert, where he might find solitude and practise fasting, strict self-discipline and prayer.

He had many imitators, in Egypt and other countries. They lived as hermits, deliberately cultivating dirt and discomfort along with religious contemplation.

One of the most notorious of such characters was Simeon Stylites. The story goes that he bound a rope around himself so tightly that it became embedded in his flesh, causing ulcers. As he moved worms dropped from him. He built a pillar sixty feet high, its flat top only a few feet in circumference. On this he stood for over thirty years, exposed to all sorts of weather. For one of those years he stood on one leg, while pilgrims from all over Europe came to admire him.

It occurs to me to wonder how Simeon lived so long without contracting either blood poisoning or pneumonia. And how was his food and drink hoisted up to him? I have a suspicion that every night, when gawping spectators departed – no doubt leaving behind a silver collection – he sclimmed smartly down the pillar, divested himself of the rope, washed off the artificial worms and had a good tuckin, prepared perhaps by his manager in a convenient cave.

In Southend there is said to be evidence that a Scottish monk – an anchorite monk according to some modern scholars – lived in a manner similar to that of Simeon Stylites. Not far from 'St Columba's Footsteps' and the Druid's Cave at Keil a small hole appears high up in the cliff-face. It can be reached, with difficulty, by a climber thrusting his way up through a narrow interior fissure which rises from the roof of a cave beneath. In the fissure, which is only about eighteen inches wide in places, are toe-holds cut into the sandstone, obviously meant to assist a climber. And on the walls of the small, flat-floored cavity behind the hole are curious marks.

Did a medieval monk once sit up there, looking out over Dunaverty Bay and contemplating the sins of the world? Nobody can be sure. What is more certain is that the hole was used as a lookout in the eighteenth century by smugglers keeping wary eyes open for the excisemen's wherry in the Sound of Sanda. Hammered deep into the rock are the remains of some rusty iron spikes. These may have supported a rope which could be used by less than expert climbers in conjunction with the toe-holds.

And the marks in the cavity above? These may have been made by watching smugglers to while away the time. They may even be natural depressions in the rock-face.

Hermit monks do not appeal to me. I would call them extremely selfish and self-centred. Saving their own souls was all they appeared to be interested in. And the devil could take the rest of the human race, for all they cared. Their holiness was not the holiness of Christ who, though ascetic enough in many respects, was also happy to live among ordinary human beings and share their enjoyment of material things.

The Rev. Stewart Mechie, in his book *Great Men and Movements in the History of the Church*, writes: 'The material side of existence is not necessarily evil: it is only evil when sought first; but in its proper subordination to spiritual purposes, it is good.' This was Christ's philosophy, in direct contradiction to that of hermit monks.

Fortunately another kind of monasticism burgeoned in the arid soil of the original. A monk called Pachomius, who at first adopted St Anthony's hermit life, became aware of its irrele-

vance in the real world. Around AD 320, in Egypt, he founded
a monastery in which monks lived as a group in a small village
consisting of individual cells. Working together they grew
their own food and made their own wine. They shared regular
hours of worship and some of them went out to preach the
gospel in nearby communities.

And Pachomius did something else which would never have
occurred to Simeon Stylites and his kind: he established a
convent for women, who also worked and worshipped
together and made missionary journeys. (I wonder how much
social contact they had with the monks. Were their prayers, by
any chance, addressed to 'Our Mother which art in Heaven'?)

This was the kind of monasticism which soon spread
throughout Europe and into Scotland, England and Ireland.
One great leader in the movement was St Martin, who lived in
the fourth century and whose name is still remembered at the
Martinmas Fair on 11 November. He was a soldier and the son
of a soldier and the hero of a legend which tells how he gave
away half of his military cloak to a shivering beggar. He
established a large monastery at Tours in France which developed into the chief training school for Celtic missionaries.
One of his students was a young man from Caledonia, the land
of the Picts and Britons, whose name was Ninian.

Not a great deal is known, historically, about Ninian,
though it is commonly agreed that he was born about the
middle of the fourth century. According to the Venerable
Bede, his father was a tribal chief in the Solway area, who had
become a Christian under the influence of the Romans. (From
the Romans Ninian's tribe of Britons had also learned new
building techniques, with stone supplanting wood, rubble and
turf, and new fish-catching techniques, some still in use today
on the shores of the Solway.)

Probably on the recommendation of his father's mentors,
Ninian journeyed to Rome, tramping south through England
and France and across the Alps like a modern hitch-hiker. An
anonymous eighth-century Latin poem tells how he saw 'milk-
white fleeces glide in the silent sky, and the mountain peaks
buried in drifts of snow'. In Rome he was 'accurately instructed' in Christian beliefs and may have encountered there
such priestly scholars as St Jerome, whose intimate knowledge

of the Bible and charismatic teaching methods made him the
William Barclay of his day, and St Ambrose, Bishop of Milan
from 374 to 397, whose reputation as a preacher had 'spread
far and wide'.

From Rome young Ninian moved on to Tours, still hiking it
along the mountain roads, but now probably in the company
of other students. There he was given a thorough grounding in
the work of mission.

Eventually, 'filled with zeal for Christ,' he came home to
Galloway about 397, bringing with him a number of followers
lent to him by St Martin. He settled in the so-called Isle of
Whithorn where, with his friends, he built a monastery – of
stone, in the Roman fashion – to which was given the name
Candida Casa (*Hwitern* or White House, afterwards
Whithorn), possibly in honour of the white hut, gifted by St
Hilary, which was the forerunner of St Martin's great estab-
lishment at Tours. And, as had been done at Tours, Ninian and
his friends grew their own food and owned cattle and horses.

It is said that Ninian himself was an enthusiastic gardener
and taught his monks how to grow leeks. (Might not their
flavour have been enhanced by the plentiful use of seaweed
from the Solway Firth?) And, what was common even among
the most saintly of early Christians, he believed in many of the
ancient superstitions. Round the monkish settlements at
Whithorn he drew mystic circles, in the manner of the Druids,
in order, as he said, to protect men and animals from the
powers of evil. (And I reckon he always transplanted his leeks
from left to right, avoiding the curse of widdershins. Some
gardening ministers of the Church of Scotland are still careful
about this.)

Today visitors come eagerly to Whithorn to see St Ninian's
Cave – where possibly he lived while Candida Casa was being
built – and the ancient sacred stones, one in the museum at
Whithorn, another two in the nearby church at Kirkmadrine.
These stones, described as 'menhirs christened with the Chi-
Ro symbol', may date back to St Ninian's time. They are
certainly among the oldest Christian relics in Britain, symbolizing the slow blood transfusion of Christianity into the
withering ancient faiths.

When St Martin died around AD 400 Ninian dedicated

Candida Casa to his old master's memory. (*Martini Laec meritus edis veneranda coruscat:* From the goodness of Martin this shrine takes its holiness and splendour.) It became *Magnum Monasterium*, 'the first university of Scotland', a centre from which a fresh impetus was given to the spread of Christianity, at first in Scotland and the north of England, then in Ireland.

Missionaries trained at *Magnum Monasterium* made their way north, spreading the good news of love among the Pictish tribes. They faced constant danger from the wolves, bears and foxes which prowled in the Caledonian Wood and from the painted barbarians who inhabited the central and north-eastern areas. But in spite of every difficulty they preached the gospel in places as far apart as Bute and Shetland, Ayrshire and Inverness-shire, where church buildings dedicated to St Ninian are still in use. And there is a tradition that it was Ninian himself who consecrated the first burial ground in Glasgow.

Almost certainly evangelizing monks from Whithorn made their way south, across the Solway and beyond Hadrian's Wall. A church at Brampton (in Cumbria), called St Martin's, provides evidence of this.

Churchmen from across the Irish Sea also came to study at *Magnum Monasterium* and on their return to Ireland worked selflessly to form the character of the Church in the 'green isle of the holiest of saints'.

Ninian died in AD 432, not long after the end of the Roman occupation. A slow death for Christianity in Scotland was also threatened about this time. In place of the reasonably civilized, cultured Romans there crashed into the south of Scotland crude, aggressive Saxons, 'carrying fire and sword and sacrilege, pulling down public and private buildings, devastating churches, breaking the sacred stones of the altars and murdering the pastors along with their flocks.'

Much of the Christian missionary work initiated at Candida Casa was undone. Many of the churches founded by Ninian and his followers were destroyed. Great numbers of Pictish converts lapsed into paganism. The barbarians took over, and for a long time it seemed as if all spiritual growth had been smothered by the weeds of aggressive materialism.

But Ninian's own Church in Whithorn survived. Churchmen from Ireland still crossed 'the narrow sea' to study at Candida Casa, and the message of love flared up strong in another place. One of those churchmen was Finnian, who later became head of the monastery at Moville (*Bun an Phobail*) in Donegal.

And one of Finnian's students was a youth named Columba, whose nickname was 'the Wolf'. Ninian's monastic ideal grew strong in his heart.

5
Distant Footsteps

A man knelt by a flat rock. It marked the western summit of a knoll above the seashore in Southend (with the hills of Ireland rising round and grey, distant only seventeen miles across the blue North Channel) at a place we now call Keil. The date was around 500 BC.

With an iron, chisel-like tool and a stone-headed hammer the man was carefully cutting a shape into the rock – the shape of a human foot. (Right foot, as it happens, size eight.) It is possible that before he began to work there had been a shallower mark upon the rock, because long before his time the knoll had been an important place in the life of the community. Some distance to the west was a cave containing a Druid altar, to the east a sacred well, with ivy growing on the rocks above it.

It is likely that the man lived with his family in or near Cnoc Araich, about a mile away. The old chief of the Epidii had died and a new chief was being chosen. Soon, according to custom, the new chief would place a foot upon the flat rock and swear faithfulness to his tribe. The man with the chisel – or his employer – had decided that a proper representation of a footprint should be made in order to emphasize the significance and dignity of the occasion. It had to be carefully aligned, in accordance with the ancient 'religious' tradition, facing due east: the east where the star Sirius rose, harbinger of the sun.

The footprint in the rock is still there. At right angles to it is another incised footprint, facing north; but according to the Royal Commission on the Ancient and Historical Monuments of Scotland this second one was cut out at a comparatively recent date. In fact, it has now partially crumbled away, leaving only the original footprint, fresh and clear, in what antiquarians might describe as mint condition. Together, they are known locally as St Columba's Footsteps.

The custom of the 'fealty foot' must at one time have been widely practised, because footsteps such as the one in Southend are to be found in many parts of Europe, particularly in the Celtic areas of Ireland and Scotland. And the custom died hard. It was still being practised by the Clan Donald as late as the fourteenth century; and a MacDonald *sennachie* (storyteller) has handed down to us a detailed description of the ceremony of proclaiming the Lord of the Isles. It contains echoes of Druidism.

'The Bishop of Argyll, the Bishop of the Isles and seven priests were sometimes present with the chieftains of the principal families. There was a square stone seven or eight feet long and the tract of a man's foot cut thereon upon which the ruler of the Isles stood, denoting that he would walk in the footsteps and uprightness of his predecessors, and that he was installed by right in his possessions. He was clothed in a white habit to show that he would be a light to his people and maintain the true religion. Then he received a white rod in his hand, intimating that he had power to rule not with tyranny and particularity but with discretion and sincerity. Next he was given his forefather's sword or some other sword, signifying that his duty was to protect and defend his people.'

It would seem that the idea behind the fealty foot was that the attributes of the old chief should be transferred to the new chief through contact, when he stood upon the exact spot on which his predecessor had stood. Is it so very different from the idea behind the 'placing on of hands' when, today, a clergyman is ordained? Such transmission of divinity runs back in time to the very hands of Christ, through St Peter.

St Columba knew all about the fealty foot.

He was born in AD 521 near Garton Lough in Donegal. His father was Felim, a chief of the royal tribe of O'Neill. His mother was Eithne, also of royal blood. No doubt when Felim was sworn in as chief he placed his foot in a carved print upon a flat rock. Both he and Eithne were described as 'royal' because they were descended from a long line of rulers, spawn of the original priestly scholars.

Their baby was born on a Thursday, 'when the tide began to flow'. A Gaelic poem, still remembered among my father's people in North Uist, runs as follows:

> Day of Columba benign:
> Day to put the web in the warp,
> To put the coracle on the brine:
> Day to hunt the heights,
> Day to put horses into harness
> And send herds to pasture.

Jean and I were married on a Thursday. So are many young couples even today, because in Scotland it is said to be a lucky day for weddings.

His parents christened him Columba, the dove. The news of Christ was now spreading throughout Ireland. The people found it happy and encouraging, because it indicated clearly, without a dictatorial edge, how peace might be found through love. Colleges and monasteries were established to train men and women as educators of willing listeners. Felim and Eithne decided that their son, in his turn, should aim to become a priestly scholar.

But as he grew up, sturdy and strong, with an imperious temper which often got him into trouble, the boys of the tribe had another name for him – Crimthann, the wolf. Love and peace were undoubtedly good things, in theory. In a world full of violence, stemming from a lust for power and influence, it was difficult in practice to establish them as a way of life.

At the age of thirteen he entered the monastery school of Doire-Eithne (founded by his mother?) in the green valley of the Leanan. Afterwards he studied at the colleges of Moville and Clonard, the Oxford and Cambridge of sixth-century Ireland. Each of them had about 3000 students, including a number of girls. (So women ministers and elders are nothing new, are they?) The professors and lecturers were all elderly men who had trained abroad as Christian missionaries, some in Europe, some at St Ninian's *Magnum Monasterium* in Galloway across the water.

At Clonard he was ordained as a priest, with the laying on of hands. But he had also learnt how to build a boat, how to construct a *bothan* (hut) with branches and clay, how to plough and sow and harvest the ripened grain. He had also acquired a taste for music and an urge to write poetry. And an oblique reference by his biographer, Adomnan, would seem to indicate that as a hurley (or shinty) player he could hit back with violence at over-enthusiastic opponents. It is, of course, not easy to maintain Christian principles when somebody hacks you on the shin with a hurley (or *caman*).

He became a worthy successor to the priestly scholars in his ancestry. His energy and leadership caused many monasteries to be founded in Ireland. Their names are like a litany: Derry and Drumhone, Durrow and Raphoe, Sords and Kells.

During all this time the dove was struggling with the wolf. Does Adomnan wish us to understand that a continuous sparking between the two poles supplied the power for a dynamic personality?

In his forty-second year the course of his life changed, a direct result of the dark urges in his character.

One of his former professors, Finnian of Moville (a product of the St Ninian tradition), came back to Ireland from a visit to Rome, carrying with him a precious manuscript, a new translation of the gospels by St Jerome. Finnian was jealous of his books and usually kept them to himself. But he made an exception in Columba's case, out of regard for his scholarship, and lent him this one on a temporary basis.

To Columba it proved so interesting that for his own use he made a copy, in secret. But Finnian found out, and the two angrily went to law about it. They appeared in court at Tara-of-the-Kings in Leinster, with Diarmit, High King of Ireland, in the judge's seat.

For many centuries Tara had been the headquarters not only of the Kings of Ireland but also of the Druids. Despite the Christian teachings so eagerly accepted by the people, the Druids still maintained an influence, especially in regard to magical and superstitious practices. Laoghaire, who had been High King of Ireland in St Patrick's day, did not accept Christianity, though he looked upon the saint's mission with tolerance and allowed his own brother, Conall – Columba's grandfather – to be baptized.

The situation in Columba's time seems to have been what modern commentators might call fluid. King Diarmit was more of a pagan than a Christian. Columba was more of a Christian than a pagan. Only gradually was the new faith being grafted on to the old, as a verse written by Columba himself shows:

> Better is he in whom we trust,
> The King who has made us all,
> Who will not leave me tonight without refuge.
> My Druid is Christ, the Son of God,
> The Son of Mary, the Great Abbot,
> The Father, the Son and the Holy Ghost.

Between Diarmit and Columba, therefore, there was antagonism on two levels: one of religious beliefs, the other concerning the 'stealing' of Finnian's book. Arguments between judge and accused promised to be long and bitter. And so it proved.

In the end Diarmit delivered judgement: a judgement, as it happens, which is the basis of our modern law of copyright: 'To every cow her calf, to every book its transcript. The copy made by you, Columba, belongs to Finnian.'

'Fury in Court' might be today's headline. Columba uttered a great and blasphemous oath. His quarrel with Finnian was forgotten. All his anger was aimed at the King. 'It is a wrong judgement!' he thundered. 'In battle will I be avenged!'

Diarmit began the Battle of Culdreimnhe (AD 562) by marching his men around an ancient chambered cairn, sunwise, from left to right, according to Druidic custom. Columba, on the other hand, blessed his followers and prayed to God for victory, though, as I study his reported words, I have the impression that his Christian conscience was troubling him and that he realized he might receive a dusty answer.

In the outcome, however, Diarmit's army was defeated. Columba's temporal power became even greater than before. His standing as a religious leader, however, was grievously compromised. His brother clerics in Ireland met in Synod at Telltown in Neath. Determined to uphold the new gospel of love and peace they accused Columba of mass murder, in that he had encouraged his followers to kill 3000 of Diarmit's men. After a trial *in absentia* he was excommunicated.

On appeal, the Synod later revoked their decision. But Columba had been taught a shattering lesson. Now penitent and grieving at the disastrous consequences of his arrogance and pride, he refused the offered mercy. He imposed sentence upon himself, and that sentence was exile. Across the narrow sea, across *Struithe na Maoile*, in the land of the Scots and Picts, he vowed to win as many souls for Christ as had fallen at Culdreimnhe. The dove had won a victory over the wolf.

Such is the story told by Adomnan and others. Details in it may be questioned by modern historians, but the important facts remain. Columba did come to Scotland. He did establish the Celtic Church in Iona. He was the greatest and most successful Christian missionary the world has known. I feel inclined to call him the angry young man of his time, who, instead of looking back in anger, now looked forward with love.

In the month of May, 563, he and twelve close friends, all clerics like himself, left Ireland in a boat built by themselves. As they sailed towards the tangled coast of Scotland Columba made a homesick poem:

> How swift is the speed of my coracle,
> Its stern turned to Derry.
> My grey eye looks back to Erin,
> A grey eye full of tears.

As I believe, they made a landing first on the shore at Keil, in Southend.

There is no documentary proof of this. But knowledgeable seamen are of the opinion that 1400 years ago anybody heading for Scotland from Derry, especially in a small boat made of wicker and hides, would never have attempted to sail north, directly to Iona, exposed all the way to the Atlantic winds and to the deadly tides which ring the Southern Hebrides. An experienced sailor, as Columba is known to have been, would have made straight for the nearest land, Kintyre.

Legend goes on to tell how Columba climbed the knoll and put his foot in the carved print on the rock and, facing east, declared himself to be a new kind of chief. Then, turning north to face the welcoming Epidii, assembled on a steep hillside which to this day is known in the Gaelic as 'the shoulder of the congregation', he explained to them how, by loving one another as Christ advised, they could find contentment and peace.

Right beside the footsteps the remains of an ancient cell are outlined beneath the turf. Was this the first crude Christian church to be built in Southend, following the Neolithic and Bronze Age cairns?

To me the legend has a clear ring of truth.

Long before Columba and his disciples scrambled ashore among its red sandstone and dolorite rocks, Keil had been a centre of religious activity. The cave with the altar is only less than a hundred metres west of the knoll; the ivy-crowned well is even closer, to the east. It seems that wherever Columba went to spread his magic – first in Ireland, then in Scotland – there in the background was an even older magic, a magic created in unrecorded time by a succession of priestly scholars.

Like Christian missionaries to African tribes in later centuries, who erected their churches near huts reputedly harbouring pagan gods, he preached his message beside the ancient cairns, the cup-marked altars and the magical Druid wells. Gradually and with courage he built a new faith on the foundation of the old. Christ, he told the Epidii, was his Druid, and on the rock above the well he carved Christ's mark, a cross. (Half the present population of Southend were baptized with water from St Columba's Well. On the cross incised above it lichen never grows. This is only to be expected, because everybody who comes to see the well instinctively traces out the cross with a finger, and so the lichen is constantly rubbed away.)

And the people found Christ's message good: a message which said that love, not worldly power, conquers all; a message which allowed them freedom from physical and mental fear.

Having established his standing among the Epidii as a new and attractive kind of leader, and having left one of his monks behind to conduct regular public worship from a little cell at Keil, Columba then travelled north to see his kinsman, Congall, Chief of the Irish immigrant clan called the Scotti, who had his headquarters at Dunadd near Lochgilhead. Or so the legend runs. From Congall he received permission to proceed to Iona, and there he finally landed with his friends, in a rocky bay still called in the Gaelic 'the port of the coracle'.

St Ninian brought Christianity to the Picts at the end of the fourth century. His efforts to establish the faith appeared, in the end, to have been thwarted. But like Montgomery after Wavell in the African desert during World War II, Columba was about to take up what Ninian had started and go on to win a victory.

By the Gaelic people Iona is called 'island of my heart' or 'island of my love', the 'heart' and the 'love' being Columba himself. After Christ, Columba is the most revered name in Hebridean culture.

On a day of sunshine Iona has a natural beauty rare in a holiday world of electric pylons, telegraph poles, caravan parks and petrol pumps. Gannets dive off-shore and wading oyster-catchers converse gravely at the edge of the white sands. Larks sing in the clear air. King-cups blossom in the marshy ground, and irises line the banks of the little streams. There is bog myrtle everywhere.

On the heathland St John's wort is plentiful. In the Gaelic its yellow flower is called 'the armpit package of Columba'. The story is that the saint always carried one inside his robe because of his admiration for John the Baptist. Poisonous ivy for the old Druids, a sweet-smelling flower for the new.

Dwarfing the ancient stones and ruins nearby, some dating back to prehistoric times, stands the modern abbey, restored and maintained by the dedicated hands of ministers and divinity students, of architects and carpenters, of masons and doctors and musicians and poets. Though the love of nature was one source of Columba's magic – as it was of Druid magic – ordinary people confused and embarrassed by so-called new moralities were also his concern.

Physically Columba was brave and strong, with a powerful voice which rang with authority. This was his birthright, perhaps. He was of royal descent. Had he not been ordained for the Church he might have become High King of Ireland. He knew how to fight with sword and shield and had once commanded an army in battle. He was so skilful a seaman that once, bringing urgent help to sick children in Jura, he sailed through the dreaded whirlpool of Corrievrechkan. But he also knew how to till the fields of Iona and how to build the cells in which he lived with his disciples. (Those cells were probably very small, constructed mainly of wood, rubble and turf. No trace of them remains.)

Morally he was brave and strong. Like David Livingstone thirteen centuries later he travelled among savage tribes with only the Cross as a talisman. He met the Druids on their own ground and by sheer force of character generally won their liking and respect. He rejected the old idea that the gods were remote and cruel and in his own life demonstrated that the Christian religion is bound up with the ordinary, everyday process of living.

Columba delighted in watching the colours of a sunset over the Atlantic. He also loved birds and animals and showed his love in a practical way. What may have been the first animal dispensary in history was in Iona, where he and his monks gave medicine to sick lambs and injured birds.

I remember a recent newspaper story about a crane with a damaged wing which made a temporary home here in Kintyre. In Iona, fourteen hundred years earlier, there was a crane with a broken leg, and Columba cured it and sent it happily on its way.

He loved wild things, but he also loved children. It was about a child that he wrote:

> O conscience clear,
> O soul unsullied,
> Here is a kiss for thee,
> Give thou a kiss to me.

He gave women an honourable place in society, raising them high on a pedestal of reverence and reminding men of the dignity of motherhood as exemplified by Mary. (The Picts may have accepted this idea without too much difficulty, because, on the whole, their society was a matriarchal one.) In Iona a lonely girl in labour called for him, and he came and held her hand and prayed for her to Christ, 'who', as he said, 'was himself a partaker of humanity'.

He was brusque and tough. He was gentle and kind. He was a warrior and a worker. But behind it all he was a poet.

He loved a ceilidh in the Iona evenings, when he sang lustily in the company of his monks and passing strangers. But in the quiet of his cell he also wrote this:

Why is there pain at the heart of a song,
Beauty that bleeds in the sweep of a hand on a harp?
Why do I search, always in vain,
For the home of my soul?
Under the sun dark is my way.
Under the moon haunted I go
By the longing that cries from the heart of a song,
The sorrow that pleads from an old man's eyes.

Was the travail of spirit which inspires a poet an important
clue to the magic influence of St Columba? Was he indicating
in these beautiful words his belief that religion, art and politics
are inextricably mixed, that there is no lasting satisfaction, no
triumph, no beauty without pain?

In his vigorous middle age he was a great traveller, with a
taste for adventure. In one of his poems he gives a picture of
himself wearing shoes made of hide and a homespun robe
belted at the waist, 'traversing corries, traversing forests,
traversing valleys long and wide'.

Adomnan tells a story of how Columba made a journey
north along the rugged western shore of Loch Ness – where he
and his two companions saw the monster – to the open
settlement which is now Inverness but which was then the
home ground of King Brudei of the Picts.

Brudei, it appears, showed considerable interest in what
Columba and his friends had to say about Christianity – even
though Briochan, the Arch-Druid, was suspicious and wanted
to send them away – and was finally won over when Columba
performed a 'miracle'.

Adomnan gives no detail about this 'miracle', except to
state, in obvious awe and wonder, that the saint 'sailed his
boat against the wind'. What was the real story?

I imagine the king as a youngish man, open minded, possibly
with an impish sense of humour. 'Columba,' I hear him say, in
Pictish words well understood by his guest, 'you argue that
Christ is more powerful than the gods of the Druids. Briochan
disagrees. Will you accept a challenge?'

Columba's whole life was a series of challenges. His re-
sponse would be immediate. 'Certainly, your Majesty!'

'Very well. Briochan declares that out there on Loch Ness he
will summon up a storm of wind from the north. He says

further that if you and your companions can sail a boat against it, he will then begin to believe in the power of this man you call Christ.'

At this point Columba may have chuckled to himself. As a weather forecaster he was as expert as Briochan. He saw furrowed clouds in the sky and knew that a strong wind from the north was likely on the following day: a natural phenomenon unrelated to any magical powers claimed by Briochan. But he also knew something that Briochan, a landlubber, did not know. A practical seaman, with sheets closehauled, can without too much difficulty sail against the wind. He, Columba, had done it a hundred times, even through the turmoil of Corrievrechkan.

And so, next day, he and his disciples cast off and tacked skilfully against the squally wind that roared down from the mountains. I like to think that, watching from the shore, Brudei laughed and thumped old Briochan on the back. 'You see, my dear Arch-Druid, he sails against the wind! His magic is stronger than yours. Mark well my words. Columba will remain here as my guest, to tell me more of Christ.'

David Hume (1711–76) defined a miracle as 'a transgression of a law of nature by a particular volition of the Deity, or by the interposition of some invisible agent'. On this basis I reckon Columba's performance on Loch Ness was no miracle. But I also believe that Adomnan had as much right to describe it as such as any present-day sub-editor searching for a headline. When a Scottish golfer won the Open Championship, for example, 'Miracle at Royal St George's' was perfectly admissible from a journalistic point of view. So, therefore, was 'Miracle on Loch Ness', because Adomnan was a journalist – and a first-class public relations officer into the bargain.

The whole incident could have been staged by that astute character, Columba himself, to impress King Brudei. What is wrong with a publicity stunt, he may have remarked to his disciples, when you have something good to sell? And proof of its efficacy was soon apparent. From that moment Druidical influence among the Picts began to crumble under the impact of Columba's message: a message which contained no threat of fear or vengeance but rather the promise of warm co-operation, neighbourliness and love.

His message also bore political fruit. The Dalriadan Scots came to an understanding with a few of the northern Pictish tribes, and Aidan, then Chief of the Scots, was elected the first king of a small area comprising modern Argyll and parts of Inverness-shire.

The crowning ceremony was performed in Iona by Columba, no doubt with considerable panache and plenty of publicity, especially for its Christian content.

As he grew older Columba's missionary journeys became less frequent. Younger monks took up the torch, travelling north into the farthest islands and south to Lindisfarne in Northumberland. He himself became thirled to a domestic routine in Iona.

It was a busy routine. 'He could not pass the space of a single hour,' wrote Adomnan, 'without applying himself either to prayer, or reading or writing, or to some manual labour.'

He and his monks held religious services every day. They studied languages: Latin and Greek, and the Gaelic they spoke in common with the Scots. One of their constant tasks was the writing and illuminating of manuscripts, mainly copies from the Scriptures, because all the churches founded by Columba on the mainland had to have service books. It could be said that Columba was one of the first publishers to operate in Scotland. (Is there anything the man couldn't do?)

They studied the stars – as all great 'religious' leaders had done before them, even back into Neolithic times – and became experts on herbs and various medicines. The monastery became a hospital for both humans and animals.

They grew barley on the *machairs* (sandy shore land) and had a seal farm which provided oil for their lamps. (Those lamps were probably *cruiskeans*, small clay or wooden receptacles shaped like sauce boats, with a wick floating in the oil which they contained. They were in use in the Hebrides and here in Southend well into the present century. Once, as a boy, I was allowed to light one for my grandmother in North Uist.)

They built boats and fished. From sheep's wool they made cloth for their robes. They made parchments for their manuscripts out of sheepskins.

They welcomed and attended to pilgrims, first washing their feet in the manner of Christ, then providing them with hospitality. Their food was barley bread, milk, fish, eggs and sometimes mutton.

They were a humble band of brothers, owning everything in common, sharing happiness and sadness. Unlike members of some monkish orders which followed them, they never kept their happy holiness to themselves. They spread it like sunshine over everyone with whom they came in contact, and, in order to do so, lived and worked as ordinary human beings.

Even in this gentle environment, however, Columba was never afraid to speak his mind. But, perhaps due to his engaging personality, nobody seems to have resented it.

On 9 June 597, at the age of seventy-six, Columba died quietly whilst engaged in copying out Psalm 34. The last words he wrote were: 'They that seek the Lord shall not lack any good thing.'

I think it is more than a coincidence that one of the lines penned by another great Scottish poet contains a similar thought. 'They never sought in vain,' wrote Robert Burns in *The Cotter's Saturday Night*, 'that sought the Lord aright.'

What is the source of St Columba's magic? Personal magnetism must be part of the answer. He was a wolf who, though striving hard to become a dove, always wore his halo at a decidedly jaunty angle, a fact which appealed greatly to ordinary sinners. But I believe the main source was his care for other people. People loved him because he loved them. And, as any honeymoon couple can testify, this is magic.

6
Love not Law

Ninian brought Christ's message and laid down the foundations of a Kirk in Scotland. The building was interrupted and
set back by barbarian violence. It did not, however, suffer
complete destruction. Builders who had been apprenticed to
Ninian spread the word in Ireland, where pagan antagonism
was less cruel. In course of time the master builder, Columba,
came from Ireland to Scotland and began the work of restoring
Ninian's edifice and establishing it as a habitable entity.

He was a Celt, a Scot, a priestly scholar, a tireless worker in
the service of Christ, a poet, a politician, a sportsman, an
animal lover. In spite of a brittle temper, which often made
him as quick to curse as he was to bless, and a lingering belief
in Druidic superstition, he had a personality which today
would probably be described as charismatic. And his qualities
of leadership, no doubt inherited from his kingly forebears,
were outstanding in his time.

Columba was perhaps fortunate that in Adomnan he had a
biographer of power and skill. Though the book dwells much
upon the saint's piety and upon the so-called miracles performed by him (most of which can be explained in a rational
way), the human side of his nature shines through on almost
every page. And Adomnan's account of the last days of
Colm-cille ('Columba of the cell', which is the Gaelic form of
Columba) has become a justly famous piece of literature.

(Samuel Johnson was fortunate, too, in having had James
Boswell, as good a writer as he was himself, to make a record
of his works and character. Sir Walter Scott had John Gibson
Lockhart to do the same for him.)

Columba was a great human being, loved and respected not
only by chieftains and kings but also by ordinary people. He

insisted that the source of Christian happiness was to be found in ordinary, everyday life: in the sound of the sea in a fisherman's ears, in the scent of fresh-turned turf in a farmer's field, in the splash of milk from a cow's udder into an earthen pail, in the giving of help, both spiritual and physical, to those in need, in the passionate embrace of a man and a maid, in the lusty cry of a new-born child. Such a message appealed to folk whose ancestors had been accustomed to regard 'religion' as a form of discipline dispensed from above, forced upon them by priestly scholars who laid down laws which were often harsh and inhuman. There was no suggestion of fear in Columba's teaching. The one requisite was that in a good world provided by God (whoever God might be) there should be love.

The Gaelic people still love Columba. He lives in their sayings, handed down from one generation to another: 'Columba the good', 'Columba, my loved one'.

Once, as a boy, I attended with my father an outdoor communion service in North Uist. The sun shone on a green hillside. The people came, walking, from far and near. They formed a hushed and eager crowd, waiting for one of the ministers to raise a hand and say, 'Let us worship God.' A scent of wild thyme, activated by the trampling of many feet, eddied about us in the salty breeze. Men and women spoke in whispers scarcely audible above the background of sea-sough and the cries of birds, but I heard one shawled old lady – a relative of my own – say to another, in the Gaelic: 'Columba of my heart is with us today.' She was a loyal Presbyterian.

Here in Southend, at the Mull of Kintyre, Columba is remembered by his 'footsteps' and by the well of clear spring water behind the churchyard. He is talked about as an old friend, with familiar warmth and affection.

The form of monasticism practised by Columba and his disciples (and by those who followed him) had nothing to do with self-succour or with the idea that religion is something apart from politics, art, sport or everyday business. It flourished best in small communities; but it aimed to spread such a message throughout the world, if that were possible. Today the trendy word is 'outreach'; and for a long time Columba's efforts at outreach were highly successful. He brought the Picts and Scots together, the catalyst being his call for peace through love. His missionaries penetrated north into what we now call the Highlands and Islands and south to Northumbria and Lindisfarne.

During this period, however, a tide of barbarism had spread across Europe into the southern parts of Britain. Scotland and Ireland were, in senses both physical and spiritual, almost completely cut off from Rome. As a consequence, the outlook and practices of the Celtic Church had developed in ways that were different from those of the Roman Church.

In the Roman Church religious ordinances were provided by priests. Monks were not concerned with this kind of work, their main preoccupation being the salvation of their own souls. In the Celtic Church the monks were all priests who cared for others and took a full part in the ordinary life of the people. In the Roman Church bishops ruled over territorial districts. In the Celtic Church divisions were tribal, the chief religious authority being the abbot of the local monastery.

Columba himself, it should be remembered, was not an abbot nor even a bishop. He called himself a presbyter, ostensibly much lower in the ecclesiastical pecking order. At the same time, by sheer force of character (and, as a true Scot, being 'a man of independent mind'), he could – and often did – tell bishops how they ought to behave in a Christian society. And he could – and did – crown a king.

Law was becoming the strong word in the Roman Church. In the Celtic Church it was individual freedom. And love.

In AD 597, the year Columba died, St Augustine came to England, an emissary of Pope Gregory, who had been much moved by the sight of some fair-haired English boys put up for sale in the Roman slave market. ('They are not Angles but angels.') From Canterbury Augustine sent out missionaries to preach Christianity among the people, who, to a great extent, had been denied any hopeful messages of love when a barbarous Anglo-Saxon rule succeeded that of the more civilized Romans.

Eventually the Augustinian missionaries, moving north, met the Columban missionaries, moving south. A conference between them was convened at Whitby, North Yorkshire, the site of a monastery founded by St Hilda in 657. (Originally Hilda was a member of the Celtic Church. But to prove that some ladies can graciously change their minds when circumstances demand a U-turn, she later lent all her considerable talent for holiness to what she called 'the Mother Church'.)

Historians seem to be uncertain about the date of this conference but agree that it took place either in 663 or 664. The deputation from Canterbury was led by Wilfrid of Ripon, that from Iona by Colman of Lindisfarne, both being abbots who afterwards became saints. The local king, Oswy of Northumbria, presided over what is now known as the Synod of Whitby. It marked the beginning of the apparently endless arguments which have gone on ever since about how the Christian Church should be organized and administered. Priestly scholars, seeking power and clamouring for law, allowed the desire of ordinary folk for love and peace to take an inferior place in their deliberations.

There was some preliminary argument about the tonsure: in other words, about how priests should have their hair cut. The Celts from Iona shaved the front part of their heads from ear to ear, reputedly in the manner of the Druids, and let their remaining hair grow long. The Anglo-Saxons from Canterbury, keeping in line with Rome, shaved the top of their heads but retained a 'coronal fringe' symbolizing the Crown of Thorns. But the principal bone of contention was the date of Easter.

The Celts calculated this by an ancient method, not unconnected with the Druidical rites of spring, which meant that they celebrated the Resurrection earlier in the year than the Anglo-Saxons. The situation had become complicated and, indeed, somewhat uncomfortable, especially at the Northumbrian court where King Oswy, a Celtic Christian, found himself observing Easter on a date differing from that of his Queen, Eanfled, who was an Anglo-Saxon Christian. Bede records the daftness of it all: 'When the king, having ended his fasting, was keeping the Paschal [Easter] Feast, the queen and her retainers would be fasting and celebrating Palm Sunday.'

Colman, a humble and unworldly man, made a humble and unworldly speech supporting the Celtic date of Easter, quoting St Columba as his principal authority. Wilfrid, more sophisticated, made a stout defence of the Roman date, quoting St Peter as his authority.

Then the bold Wilfrid uttered words which have been echoed in various ways throughout succeeding centuries: words which indicate that even as early as the seventh century the people of South Britain imagined they were in all respects superior to those in the North. He told Colman and his Columbans: 'Even if your fathers were true saints, surely a small company on a corner of a remote island is not to be preferred to the blessed Church of Christ.'

From what was Iona remote? Not from heaven, I suggest. And was Columba's Church not as blessed and as much of Christ as that of Rome? It occurs to me to wonder if Wilfrid's arrogant statement might have produced the first fertile seeds of Scottish Nationalism.

As president, King Oswy now discovered – somewhat to his discomfort, I imagine – that he had to give a decision: Easter according to the Celts or Easter according to the Anglo-Saxons. Like many a good man before and since he reckoned that harmony in his home and his kingdom was to be preferred to continuous argument. Consequently he made a judgement which he knew would please his Anglo-Saxon wife and, at the same time, consolidate his own power in Northumbria, where the invading Anglo-Saxons had acquired more political clout than the original Celtic inhabitants.

Such considerations, of course, were not specially mentioned in his summing up. Coming down on the side of Wilfrid and declaring that the date of Easter should be calculated according to Roman custom, he gave what may appear to be a rather selfish reason, one cooked up perhaps by his public relations people: 'St Peter is the door-keeper,' he said, unctuously, 'whom I will not contradict . . . lest when I come to the gates of the kingdom of heaven there should be none to open them, he being my adversary who is proved to have the keys.' How many Celts since then have considered their own mental and physical comfort to be more important than that of the spiritual health of their Celtic fellows?

On the surface the Synod of Whitby was mainly about tonsures and the date of Easter. In truth it was about the very framework and discipline of the Church.

Afterwards, though only gradually, the 'rustic simplicity' (as Wilfrid called it) of the Celtic Church, its concern for the spiritual well being of ordinary people and the lack of desire on the part of its leaders for material possessions was submerged under mighty waves from Canterbury and Rome, whose priestly scholars now argued that the cause of Christ could best be advanced by colourful ceremonies, by the acquisition of splendid retinues and, above all, by their own co-operation with powerful secular rulers. The Roman priests and prelates made no reference, of course, to the fact that such a policy contributed greatly to their own worldly advancement.

Columba believed that the strength of the Church was to be found in lowly communities of pious people reaching out and influencing each other. The Church of Rome believed that it was to be found in groups of powerful leaders who could lay down and enforce the law. In other words, the Celtic Church tended to be democratic, that of Rome dictatorial.

That such a divide should be blamed upon superficial arguments relating to tonsures and the date of Easter is typical of what has always gone on in the Church. When Christ's teachings threaten the worldly position of a political party, a business concern or a greedy individual, superficial arguments of emotional appeal to tribal and nationalistic loyalties are frequently deployed to camouflage and bedevil the main issue. Even lingering pagan beliefs can be brought into play, as happened in 1984, when the lightning strike on York Minster was said to indicate God's wrath at the Bishop of Durham's intellectual views upon the Resurrection and the Virgin Birth.

The complete irrelevance to Christianity of many a 'religious' argument is well illustrated by the apparently everlasting one about the date of Easter. By simple, unscholarly souls – among whom I count myself – the question is continually asked: why does the date of Easter move about so much, while that of Christmas does not?

In the years after the death of Christ it appears that some confusion occurred between Easter and a pagan spring festival which took place at the vernal (spring) equinox: a festival which celebrated Eostre, the Teutonic goddess of dawn. There was confusion also between Easter and the Jewish Passover. As a consequence, the early Church got in a muddle about the appropriate date and the arguments began: arguments which still run in full spate.

In parts of the Middle East the church quietly decided to celebrate Easter on the 14th of Nisan (approximately our month of April), whatever the day of the week. This was in line with the date of the Jewish Passover which commemorated – and still commemorates – the destruction of the first-born of the Egyptians and the 'passing over' of the Israelites by the destroying angel. The decision was supported by many contemporary authorities, including St Melito of Sardis, fragments of whose writing (on papyrus) can be seen at the University of Michigan.

Then, around 190, Pope Victor put a cat among the cooing pigeons. He declared that the date of Easter should be arrived at in accordance with the phase of the moon at the time of the vernal equinox. He told the Quatrodecimanists (the fourteenth-day people) that they must accept his ruling and, indeed, excommunicated one Quatrodeciman bishop who tried to argue with him.

The question then arose: should Easter be held before or after the vernal equinox? The three principal cities of the Roman empire, Rome, Antioch and Alexandria – all had their own astronomers, each group with their own calculating system and each offering a different answer. This led to further and even more bitter disputes. Which group of astronomers was right?

Eventually, in 325, the Council of Nicaea was convened, under the presidency of the Emperor Constantine himself. One of its purposes was to clarify the situation in regard to Easter. It came to the conclusion that the Alexandrian system was the best and that Easter should be dated by the behaviour of the moon *after* the vernal equinox.

The Roman Church in Britain fell into line. And slowly, following the Synod of Whitby, so did an unwilling Celtic Church which, until then, isolated and independently minded as it was, had been celebrating Easter on dates which possibly had an origin in Druidical custom.

An effort to appoint a fixed day for Easter was made in 1582, when Pope Gregory introduced a new calendar to supersede the Julian calendar (named after Julius Caesar). But after much fuming and fussing it was agreed that to interfere with an old custom would be a bad thing. The date of Easter would continue to be determined by the moon. A moon, let it never be forgotten, which was not a real moon but an imaginary one.

At this stage you may be feeling as muddled and as frustrated as I am. But an end to this chronicle of daftness is not yet even in sight.

From the twelfth century to the mid-eighteenth century England had persisted in using the Julian Calendar. Its New Year started on 25 March, the feast of the Annunciation of the Blessed Virgin (Lady Day). Meanwhile the Scots, true to their independent spirit, had been using a calendar of their own, based partly on Pope Gregory's and partly on a tradition with roots possibly in the Neolithic Age. Their New Year's Day occurred in mid-January.

Now, however, in 1751, the British Parliament decided to adopt the Gregorian calendar in a pure and unadulterated form and passed 'An Act for Regulating the commencement of the year; and for correcting the Calendar now in use'. It said that the existing calendar (i.e. the Julian calendar) 'hath been found by Experience to be attended with divers inconveniences'. For example, the fact that 'Scotland and other Nations' kept 'different years' had hindered the export trade. And trouble had been encountered in the dating of deeds and other documents. The Act also pointed out that the Julian calendar, for astronomical reasons, was 'erroneous': the Julian year of 365 days was eleven minutes and ten seconds too long and the vernal equinox which in 325 had been on or about 25 March, was now occurring on 9 or 10 March. And, it added ominously, the 'said error is increasing'. In simple terms, the Julian calendar had fallen out of kilter with what was actually going on in the natural universe.

It was, in fact, eleven days out of kilter. The 1751 Act, therefore, laid down that in England and Scotland the year 1752 should start on 1 January and lose eleven days in September: 2 September, it said, would be followed immediately by 14 September. Riots occurred in London at the time and crowds marched on Westminster, shouting: 'Give us back our eleven days!' But since the succeeding years still contained 365 days, with a day added every four years, the days 'lost' were lost only in the mind. Their sequence had merely been adjusted so that the calendar might not fall out of step with the seasons.

Having fixed up a new year, the sponsors of the 1751 Act were faced with the problems of fixing Easter, since the vernal equinox was now occurring on a different date.

(I hope you are following all this. I think I am, though with considerable difficulty.)

One interesting detail which emerges from a study of the Act is that in 1751, not long after the Union, the British Parliament freely acknowledged the fact that Scotland is a 'Nation' in its own right: not a 'Region', as some modern bureaucrats so often mistakenly describe it.

With the help of astronomers and scientific advisers – and by bringing Golden Numbers and Sunday Letters into play – elaborate rules and tables were drawn up and attached to the statute: rules and tables which calculated the date of Easter up to the year 2199. A footnote was added, which, I believe, justifies the title of this book: 'Ecclesiastical Full Moons do not fall on the same day as real Full Moons.'

These are the rules and tables, having nothing at all to do with Christianity, which still legally determine the Sunday on which Easter falls.

Several moves have been made towards fixing an immovable Easter.

Shortly after World War II the League of Nations recommended that it should be celebrated on the first Sunday after the first Saturday in April. But like many another good idea put forward by the League of Nations it was lost in a welter of petty disputation among secular rulers and priestly scholars, most of them believing their own pride and prestige to be far more important than the well being of their people.

On 15 June 1928 an Easter Bill to fix a date was put before Parliament at Westminster. A moving date, its supporters said, was inconvenient for schools, the 'commercial classes', the railways and tourists and holidaymakers. And one sensible and practical MP suggested to the House that a late Easter might ensure better weather for the holidays.

Originally the Bill made no mention of Christianity or of

any Church. Eventually, however, it was changed so that before the date was fixed the Christian Churches had to be consulted and their views taken into account.

The Act was passed. But since then nothing has happened. Why? Simply because Parliament, when it consulted them, found that 'the Christian Churches' could not agree amongst themselves — not for the first time, I fear, nor for the last — upon a fixed date for Easter. And Parliament is unwilling to make any move until 'the Christian Churches' give it a unanimous go-ahead.

For years the World Council of Churches has been trying to achieve consensus on this subject among its members. But though the British and the Roman Catholic Churches appear to be in favour of a fixed Easter the Orthodox Church is not. Recently a bishop of the Orthodox Church said: I see no virtue in the Church changing. The cycles of the moon are very important for our lives, though urban man may not be conscious of them. To fix Easter would show a loss of awareness, a lack of sensitivity to these matters. It is not a matter of faith, but of traditional custom.'

. It appears, therefore, that we could have a fixed Easter tomorrow if it wasn't for the Orthodox Church and its strict adherence to the decisions of the Council of Nicaea in 325.

Old Alec Soudan was a jobbing gardener in Southend when I was an adolescent. He had what he called a 'silver ja' ', the result of a grievous face wound received in World War I. The movable Easter caused him irritation and confusion, because he believed, on vaguely religious grounds, that Easter was the best day on which to plant late potatoes, amongst them the magnificent Golden Wonders with which he sometimes provided us at Achnamara.

On one occasion, when Easter occurred in March, he found the weather at the time to be cold, damp and unfavourable for planting; but he went ahead with the job even against his natural instinct. The result was that in April, when his seed potatoes should have been snugly underground, tender young growth had appeared. This was scourged by a night of severe frost, followed by a gale, and the crop ruined.

Alec looked at me with lugubrious eyes: 'Why can they no'

fix Easter on the same day every year? What the hell does it maitter at whit time o' year Jesus rose frae the deed, sae lang as he did — an' the weans [children] can sing "Jesus loves me"?'

7
Stone of Destiny

With its direction and organization at least under the influence of Rome, the Church in Scotland seemed to have a reasonably bright future.

There was a good supply of priestly scholars – in monasteries, 'colleges' and parochial areas – to keep loving and sometimes stern eyes on religious affairs. But in time, as the European authorities showed little interest in Scotland and made no attempt to exercise jurisdiction over it, the priestly scholars tended to ally themselves more and more with the secular rulers, a practice which may have been to their own material advancement but was certainly detrimental to the general welfare of the people.

Among the Scots there was little national feeling or, indeed, spiritual cohesion. Life for ordinary folk was at a level of existence rather than of well being. There were no towns, no urban communities. People's lives were spent in scrabbling for food in the wilderness, in hunting for fish and protecting their families from wild animals, in keeping their dwellings under repair and in fighting off neighbouring tribes who threatened to invade their home ground. At a higher level fighting still went on among the Picts in the north and east and the Scots in the west and south.

Despite every difficulty, however, Christ's message of love and peace did spread out and find a way into the hearts of some secular rulers and, through the missionary monks, to some of the people. A few dedicated priestly scholars, now unknown, must have done a good job for Christianity in spite of Rome's indifference and a local background of social incoherence.

The situation became even more incoherent when the pagan

Norsemen came to raid and plunder and, eventually, to settle in Shetland and Orkney, in the Hebrides and on the western mainland. Contrasting with Norway, which was overpopulated, Scotland provided them with plenty of living room; and the land, though difficult enough to cultivate, was less barren than that of their home country. In the late ninth century, according to the *Laxdaele Saga*, one of their number 'decided to go west across the sea to Scotland because . . . he thought it would be good living there. He knew the country well, for he had raided there extensively.'

At first, during the raiding period, the Norsemen dealt cruelly with the Christians among the Picts and Scots. Iona was laid waste three times; and in 825 Abbot Blathmae and his monks were massacred at the altar for refusing to betray the hiding place of the precious shrine which contained the bones of St Columba. But gradually, down the passing years, as the raiders became settlers, sowing barley and oats and breeding sheep and cattle, there occurred a certain peace. Intermarriage with the Picts and Scots took place. The majority of the pagan Norsemen became Christian.

Part of the reason for this, according to my Hebridean ancestors, was that when a Norseman married a local girl she kept the Columban spirit of Christian love alive by transmitting it in song and story to their children. My grandmother in North Uist once said to me: 'Ay, Angus, you are tall and fair. You have the Norse blood in you. But – thanks be to the womenfolk among your forebears – you have the love of Christ in your heart and not the fear of Thor and Odin.'

The first cathedral in Scotland was built in the eighth century on the Brough of Birsay. On this small island at the north-west tip of Orkney the remains of Earl Thorfinn's Hall can still be seen, among other Norse, Christian, Celtic and prehistoric ruins. St Magnus was originally buried there.

In the twelfth century his nephew, Earl Rognvald, built a cathedral in Kirkwall. He took his uncle's bones from the Brough of Birsay, buried them on the site, and called it the Cathedral of St Magnus. Lovingly and splendidly restored in recent times, it is now a parish church within the Presbyterian government of the Scottish Kirk. Its history contains, in essence, all the elements in the evolution of the Church of Scotland during the past 5000 years.

In Southend, too, memorials of the Norse occupation are to be found.

Many of our place names are purely Norse. The looming headland immediately east of the Mull of Kintyre is called Borgadaile, which derives from *Borgar-dal-r*, meaning the glen of the fort. High above the glen in question the well preserved remains of an Iron Age *dun* are prominent on a rocky bluff overlooking the sea. Then there is the old name for Sanda, the spoon-shaped island which I can see from my window, across the grey Sound. Until early in the nineteenth century Sanda's map-name was Avon, from the Norse word for a haven. No doubt the Norwegian long-ships often sheltered in its comfortable harbour, as do storm-caught yachtsmen to this day.

Other names, however, are hybrids – part Norse, part Gaelic. They reveal how the invaders, instead of destroying the native Gaelic culture, were gradually absorbed into it.

Richard and Elizabeth Semple, our farming neighbours (who supply us with dung for our garden, in return for a few vegetables in season), live at Low Cattadale, a perfect example of a place-name made up of Gaelic and Norse, with a small sprout of modern English.

'Catta' is derived from Catherine, a Gaelic saint who had her cell in the area. The 'dale' is Norse for a vale or valley.

Another Southend hybrid is Dalvraddan, a farm name which means the valley of the *bhradain* or salmon. Yet another is the eminence of Rhu Stafnish, on our eastern shore, a friendly landmark to seamen and airmen because of the radio guidance mast on its summit. Rhu, in Gaelic, means 'the headland of the precipice'. Stafnish, in the Norse form *Stafa-nes*, means exactly the same. I can imagine a meeting of Gaels and Norsemen trying to decide upon a name for the place. Neither side is willing to give way. 'Ach, to hell with it! Let us call it both!' 'Ya, ya, my friend. A good compromise. After all, what is in a name?'

On the machair, just above the yellow sand-line beyond Pennyseorach farmhouse (roughly a mile and half along the coast from Achnamara) there stands a squat stone pillar known in Southend as the Rat Stane. It is about a metre high, with its top hollowed out in the shape of a font. Old Hugh MacEachran, Kirk Treasurer in my father's time, who was a fount of parish lore, used to tell me that 'frae the Rat Stane tae the Gull's Face' – a cliff which shelters the harbour in Sanda – 'is exactly twa mile'. It has always been a favourite rendezvous for young lovers (such as Jean and myself sixty years ago) in search of romantic seclusion, where the soft sough of the sea and the whisper of a breeze among the bent are undisturbed by any dance or disco beat.

Not so long ago, in the spring, tenants of Pennyseorach Farm used to place a pin or other metal object in the 'font' so that their fields might be fruitful and their cattle fertile in the coming year. Sandy Ronald, who farmed Pennyseorach more than half a century ago, once showed me numerous small rust marks in the 'font'. They had been made, he said, by nails and pins left there in previous years by his ancestors. And by himself. He was, let it be noted, a staunch member of the Kirk.

The roots of the 'sacrificial' superstition are clear enough. They go back thousands of years into prehistory, even as far back, perhaps, as the Mesolithic Age. But what is the significance of the word 'Rat'?

The suggestion has been made that here is another of the common 'Wratty Stanes', associated with the cure of warts. But no local tradition of such a kind exists. I would say that in this case 'Rat' is derived from a Norse word meaning 'meeting place' (*cf.* the German *Rat-haus*, or Town Hall). The stone with the chiselled out 'font' may originally have been pagan, re-erected in early Christian times: nearby is the farm of Kilmashenachan, the cell or church of St Sennachan. But when the Norsemen came may they not have used it as a meeting place for the conduct at first of councils of war and, later perhaps, of peace?

The Rat Stane and the place-names are the only evidence remaining of a Norse presence in Southend. It shows, I think, how thoroughly the strangers were integrated into the Gaelic community, not only in my parish but throughout the west and north of Scotland.

Thor and Odin were forgotten, their harshness smoothed away and softened by the gentle magic of love.

*　　　*　　　*

The Scots Kirk (*Ecclesia Scoticana*) is first documented as such in 878. In spite of the Norse invasions and the constant battles for power between Pictish and Scottish tribes, the Christian faith was gradually spreading among the people, in much the same way as it is still doing among the warring tribes of Africa and Central America today. And the organized Church, though still not fully thirled to Rome, was putting down stronger and stronger roots. Gradually, too, as rich humus does when added year after year to a sandy garden, the Scots, heirs to Columba, were becoming the predominant element in their political mix with the Picts, the Norsemen and the Anglo-Saxons.

Like many another amateur historian before me – and like many a professional one, too, it appears – I founder somewhat helplessly in the morass of Scottish history during this period: a history in which Church and State – as always in Scotland – are inextricably mingled. But among the quaking tussocks of knowledge there are some, I think, upon which I can rest a fairly confident foot.

In the sixth century St Columba's dream had been of Scots and Picts united in a Christian Celtic kingdom. He did not live to see his dream come wholly true. But events continued to occur which slowly but surely brought it to a stage of reality.

In the west the Scots were being harassed by Scandinavian marauders from the north. In the east the Picts were being harassed by Anglian marauders from the south. The Scots were not able to oust the Norsemen; they absorbed them instead. The Picts dealt much more dramatically with the Anglians. In 685, at the Battle of Nechstansmere (near Forfar in Angus) they won a famous victory over King Egbrith's army, sending it back to England 'to think again'.

In the ninth century the leader of the Scots (and of some of the Picts) was Kenneth MacAlpin. He had been forced to leave his capital in the west – Dunstaffnage near Oban – by the press of Norse influence in that area. He moved his headquarters east to Scone (Perthshire), bringing with him, for safe keeping against possible Norse depredation, some relics of St Columba which, until then, had been kept in Iona.

One of those relics, I suspect, was the rough-hewn stone on which King Aidan had sat more than two centuries before during his coronation by Columba. By us, the Scots, lovers of words and sounds of a dramatic sort, it is called the Stone of Destiny. (As far as our national aspirations are concerned much good it has done us.)

For some time Kenneth had been waging war against certain Pictish tribes, his intention being to create a united – and much larger – Kingdom of Scotland. But it was love, not violence, which eventually brought him a measure of success. He married a Pictish princess, and in the euphoria of this union the majority of the Picts and Scots decided that they, too, should unite, with Kenneth as their king.

He was crowned King of Alba in 834, at Scone, upon the Stone of Destiny which some say is the veritable stone upon which Queen Elizabeth II of England and I of Scotland was crowned in Westminster Abbey in 1953. (The origins of the famous stone are obscure, though I should think that at an early date it was brought from Ireland by the *Scotti* for use in tribal ceremonies. It is possible, incidentally, that the stone now in Westminster Abbey is not the original one but simply a chunk of ordinary Perthshire rock.)

Kenneth MacAlpin made practical Columba's vision. And the new king did not forget to honour the old prophet. He rebuilt in his memory the cathedral church of Dunkeld (not far from Scone) and named the first Abbot of Dunkeld successor to Columba and Head of the Church in the new, emerging nation.

In 1985 I spoke in the cathedral during the Dunkeld and Birnam Arts Festival. It was a thrilling experience. I had come from Southend at the Mull of Kintyre, where it is probable that Columba first set foot in Scotland. Now I was here, where his dream of a Christian kingdom had been realized, if only in a tenuous way: where, according to ancient 'religious' rites, Kenneth MacAlpin had been married to a land peopled by both Picts and Scots, seated upon a stone symbolic of that land.

The Cathedral of Dunkeld – like the Cathedral of St Magnus in Orkney – is now a Presbyterian Kirk in the body of the Church of Scotland. That morning I was proud that I, no priestly scholar, should be allowed, from the chancel, to address my fellows in a spirit of democracy. But I was aware also of echoes in the vaulted roof: echoes of ancient strivings to find God, not altogether for the sake of the people but in order to enhance the power of ancient kings.

Outside the cathedral, in the fresh landscape of river, blossoming trees and lush green fields, there are the tall stones of the Neolithic Age; there are Bronze Age cairns and Iron Age *duns*. I was aware, that bright Sunday morning, that our grasp of Christianity is still uncertain, the truth only perceived perhaps, through a glass darkly.

In the days of the tall stones and the bronze implements of war 'religion' was dictated to the people from the top. Inspired by Christ's teaching, St Ninian and St Columba had attempted to change all that, allowing ordinary men and women to find, in the life and work of their own communities, the love and peace for which they longed. But as the Church became organized on a national level, and as local chiefs became kings of wider domains, the 'religion' of the country, though still ostensibly Christian, tended again to be used as an instrument of secular power.

No doubt many of the rulers who wielded such power were good and sincere, eager to bring love and peace to their subjects. But as had probably happened before in prehistoric times, their love of power grew stronger than their love of people. 'Human nature is gey ill [difficult] tae turn,' as old Alec used to say. The kings and the priestly scholars believed that they knew best how to spread the gospel and became especially enamoured of the text 'Render unto Caesar the things which are Caesar's.'

In the ninth century Dunkeld succeeded Iona as the Celtic capital of Scotland. In the tenth century the leadership of the Church passed to St Andrew's, an old religious foundation revered because of the legend that 'an arm bone, three fingers, a tooth and a knee-pan' of St Andrew were buried there. Since then St Andrew has been Scotland's patron saint and her flag the white diagonal St Andrew's cross on a blue background.

Kenneth MacAlpin's successors as rulers of Scotland were appointed by the ancient Celtic law of tanistry. This implied that the heir to the throne should be named in the king's lifetime as the individual best fitted for the high office. He was always of the blood royal, usually a brother, cousin or nephew of the king. Such a system led to much jealousy, political manoeuvring, violence and murder.

One glaring example of this occurred in the eleventh century when the ageing Macbeth, who had a claim in tanistry to the throne, saw that he had little chance of living long enough to succeed the young king, Duncan, and proceeded, therefore, to kill him in battle.

When he became king, Macbeth did not prove to be the weak and nasty creature depicted by Shakespeare. He ruled wisely and reasonably well for seventeen years and, it has been suggested, was able to spread a sense of national unity in both the far north and far south of Scotland. He was also generous to the Church and made a pilgrimage to Rome somewhere around 1050.

Was the pilgrimage, I wonder, partly a public relations exercise and partly, in view of his guilty conscience, a kind of insurance policy in support of his immortal soul?

King Duncan was a direct descendant of Kenneth MacAlpin, probably in the seventh generation. When he was killed by Macbeth his son, Malcolm, aged nine, had been sent for safety to the English court of Edward the Confessor. Malcolm considered Macbeth a murderous usurper and grew up intent upon revenge. In 1058 he invaded Scotland with an English army recruited in Northumbria and killed Macbeth at the Battle of Lumphanan, north-west of Aberdeen. To make sure of his own and his descendants' future grip on the Scottish throne, he slaughtered Macbeth's family as well.

When it came to the acquisition of temporal power, the Christian gospel of love would seem to have had small influence upon the actions of our ancestors. But were those actions any less savage than those of our contemporaries in Ireland, Europe, India, Africa, Central America, the Middle East, the Far East and at certain football grounds? Some power-crazy politicians and profit-crazy industrialists (especially the arms manufacturers), are still doing their best to demonstrate that a universal acceptance of 'love thy neighbour' is still an almost impossible dream.

Historically known as Malcolm III, the new king was also called Malcolm Canmore by the people of Scotland. ('Big head' may be a literal translation of the Gaelic *Cean Mor*, but the nickname actually means 'Great Chief'.) His first wife was Ingibjorg, a Norse lady whose father was Earl of the Orkneys.

In 1069, after Ingibjorg died, leaving him with three young children, he married a second wife. This was Margaret, who was English and for a time had been at the court of Edward the Confessor. When the Norman Conquest took place (even I know that date without recourse to a reference book) she had fled with her family to Scotland – to the Scottish court at Dunfermline – and had there met and caused Malcolm to fall in love with her.

It can be said that it was Margaret's influence, as queen, which brought about two far-reaching changes in the character of both the Scottish State and the Scottish Church. The old system of tanistry was submerged under new legislation. Englishmen and Normans were given lands in Scotland and a feudal system of land tenure was introduced, bringing some order to the near tribal chaos. The Celtic Church, still clinging nostalgically to certain aspects of Columban love and freedom, was brought firmly and finally under the direct legal sway of Rome.

I have a tremendous admiration for Queen Margaret's character. She was a model wife and mother and made Malcolm's home more comfortable than it had been and his court more dignified. She possessed intense religious fervour and had a complete devotion to what she conceived to be her duty. Bishop Turgot, who died in 1115, wrote her biography. 'Of all living persons whom I know or have known,' he said, 'she was the most devoted to prayer and fasting, to works of mercy and almsgiving.'

Unlike her husband, the king, who lacked education – except perhaps in the arts of war, murder and political infighting – she could read the Bible and the works of the priestly scholars in Latin.

Her personality was strong, much stronger than that of her husband. As Turgot reveals, Malcolm had 'a sort of dread of offending her'. He could not read the books which she studied, but he would handle them with reverence and even awe, kiss the covers and have them ornamented with precious stones for her. Remembering how, in his early years, he had killed

Macbeth and Macbeth's family, was he now, I wonder, trying to salve a guilty conscience?

Margaret was strong for the well being of the Church: not the Church as she found it in Scotland but the orthodox Church of Rome. Amid plenty of publicity, she did her best to prove that she also had the well being of the people at heart.

She donated Malcolm's money and even some of his property to various 'Christian' causes. She showed great sympathy for hermits and pilgrims, though not much for the Culdees, monks who still followed some of the beliefs and practices of the old Celtic Church. (Her sons, Alexander I and David I, eventually suppressed the Culdees altogether.) English slaves were ransomed. Rich vessels and embroidery were presented to various churches. Beggars were received at court, and before an admiring audience she herself knelt down and washed their feet.

That is Bishop Turgot's story. He does not actually say that she lectured everybody in sight as to how they ought to behave. But he does suggest that she emphasized to all her subjects the supreme importance, as far as their souls' salvation was concerned, of putting aside the cultural heritage of the Celtic Church and obeying strictly the dictates of Rome. She travelled the country making it plain to them that she regarded non-churchgoing as an evil that could – and must – be eradicated.

On the whole I get the impression of Margaret as the supreme do-gooder. But like certain rampant women in our modern scene, imposing upon others their own conception of moral and material values, it seems to me that she lacked some of the more humble and lovable human qualities: the qualities possessed, for example, by a Mother Teresa.

It makes me feel guilty, however, just to contemplate the wide scope of Margaret's holiness. It makes me feel guilty, too, to realize that I am basically prejudiced against her because she so strenuously supported not only the Roman Church but also the Anglo-Saxon and Norman ideas of government.

She died in Edinburgh in 1093, not long after the death of her husband, who was killed – along with their eldest son – while fighting against marauders from England.

Quarrelling, fighting, killing.

For ordinary Scots people, longing for love and peace, there was still no spiritual rest, no material security. They were told how to be holy, how to obey the laws of God as interpreted by Rome. But they were still forced to ignore such laws when ordered to fight – and sometimes die – for their masters' dictatorial ambitions.

8
Seeds of Independence

In the years following Queen Margaret's death the Church in Scotland gradually became better organized and more richly endowed. But the Christian message of brotherly love, of freedom in thought and action, still brought little benefit to ordinary people, who had no say in the work of the Church. It was obscured and even choked almost out of existence by the burgeoning foliage of 'holy' ideas emanating from Rome, which laid more emphasis upon elaborate ritual than upon the spiritual and material care of individuals.

Perhaps such ritual appeared to be necessary at the time. Ordinary folk were uneducated, unable to read or even to understand what was said at the Church services, which were always conducted in Latin. Church authorities may have come to the conclusion that the Christian message should be conveyed to ignorant people through the senses: by the reverent movements of the priest, by lights gleaming on expensive vessels around the altar, by the smell of incense. But this was an altogether different approach from that of the old Celtic Church whose ministers had lived and worked among the people and demonstrated the love of Christ in their own everyday actions.

The situation was like that in television today, where many plays are so elaborately mounted and so brilliantly acted and produced that what the writers have to say is often obscured and appears to be of secondary importance.

Margaret's sons, Alexander I (1107–24) and David I (1124–53) continued her work in Scotland of establishing Roman law in the Church and Anglo-Norman ideas in government.

On the ecclesiastical side the country was divided into

dioceses and bishoprics, each diocese with its cathedral (principal church) in which a bishop had his *cathedra* or chair. He was assisted in his work of Church government by clergymen called deans and canons who also lived at the cathedral and formed a 'chapter'.

The dioceses were divided into parishes, each with its own priest. Those priests did all the pastoral work now done by ministers, except preaching. This was always done by the bishops or by visiting friars.

It was all a kind of holy version of the feudal system which was also being established on Norman foundations.

David I gave large amounts of money and land to the Church: so much money and land, indeed, that he impoverished his successors to the throne.

> He illumined in his days
> His lands with kirks and with abbeys.

In the architecture of those abbeys and kirks Norman influence was strong. It can be found, for example, in St Margaret's Chapel in Edinburgh Castle and in the ruins of Dunfermline Abbey. It can also be found in part of the ancient ruins of St Columba's Chapel in the churchyard at Keil, Southend, a short, after-breakfast walk from my front door.

Often, when bemused by history, I go inside this narrow, roofless building, where I listen in quietness to the sound of the wind and the sea outside and allow the scent of wet earth and grass to eddy round me.

Sometimes the therapy is successful: I glimpse an unsophisticated, near to nature pattern which, almost imperceptibly, is growing bigger and richer as the troubled years, centuries and millennia go by.

At other times, as the stone walls with their empty lancet windows lean and leer above me, I become depressed by the thought of how so often in the past – and in the present – men themselves have disturbed the pattern by allowing hate, arrogance, ambition for power, selfishness, pomp and gaudy circumstances to smother the simple, true meaning of 'love thy neighbour'.

Part of the old chapel dates back to the thirteenth century. It is small, a claustrophobic rectangle built of sandstone and rubble, approximately nine metres by six metres. It never had seats. Worshippers, who must have been few, stood or knelt on the earthen floor as a priest in coloured vestments intoned services in Latin.

The majority of such worshippers were probably of the lesser 'nobility' in the district. Their overlords and their kings and queens were, in the main, all supporters of the Church, as a rule because bishops, familiar with Latin and having some knowledge of other countries, often proved useful, in political terms, as advisers and ambassadors. It would be to the advantage of local leaders, therefore, to be known as supporters, too. They might understand little of what the priest was saying, but he would create an atmosphere redolent of the hope of heaven and the fear of hell, and their thoughts, therefore, would be directed towards the necessity of doing good deeds in this world in order to ensure comfort for their souls in the next.

No doubt a few of their good deeds would concern the well being of their employees. But not a lot. Little was done for the education of ordinary folk. (Little was done, either, for the education of the 'nobility', except in warlike pursuits like archery, swordsmanship and horsemanship.)

Tradesmen – masons for example, stone carvers and carpenters – were encouraged and did much fine work; but in many country districts the life of the workers was crude and miserable. Conscientious priests did their best to care for them, offering baptism (and confirmation by bishops), marriage ceremonies, extreme unction for the dying and solemn funeral services. Some taught their parishioners to repeat the Lord's Prayer, the Apostles' Creed and the Ten Commandments. And they saw to it that holidays were given at Christmas, Easter and other Holy Days upon which saints might be commemorated.

But in spite of such efforts on the part of the Church (mainly by the parish priests) quarrelling and fighting still went on among the nobility; ordinary folk had little sense of peace and security.

The times were so violent, indeed, as kings and nobles and landowners struggled for power and influence, that many people, sickened by the 'rat-race', chose to take refuge from it by entering one of the many monasteries which Queen Margaret and her sons had favoured and had caused to be built. They became monks, rejecting earthly ties and earthly wickedness, intent upon the saving of their own souls. In this they differed entirely from the monks of the Celtic (Columban) period, who had ministered to the people among the people and who had cared for the spiritual well being of the people as much as for their own. It was a return to the narrow, selfish days of St Anthony and Simeon Stylites.

Those Scottish monasteries were of various orders. The one at Dunfermline was Benedictine, the one in Arbroath Tironesian. Newbattle Abbey was Cistercian, Cambuskenneth Augustinian. The Abbey in Kintyre, at Saddell, some twenty-five miles north of Southend, was Cistercian. They were established by monks, friars, nuns, templars, all abjuring the life and habits of the sinful world outside. In theory, that is.

The abbeys were certainly peace-loving and, in certain ways, specially useful. Some of them — Kelso, for example — were large estate owners, with tenants on their farms. They also employed many secular shepherds for their secular sheep.

Monks were under an oath of obedience to 'superiors'. They were supposed to follow rules of individual poverty and of purity in mind and action. By outsiders — kings and commoners alike — they were much esteemed for their ascetic life, and I have no doubt that many a saintly soul existed in their midst. The idea flourished that no one could be a real Christian unless he or she left the world and took monastic vows. When somebody entered a monastery it was said that he or she had been 'converted'.

No matter how hard I try, I cannot banish the thought that such over-indulgence in 'holiness' leads to intellectual constipation. Christianity does not mean a hiding away from sin and suffering, a selfish caring for one's own soul and let the devil take everybody else's. Christianity is not in-bred. It has a care for all mankind and is eager to take a full part in the hurly-burly of existence — among saints and sinners, rich and poor, the healthy and the sick, among doctors trained to save life and weapon manufacturers trained to destroy it, among

soldiers and sailors and airmen employed by politicians to
fight battles and kill one another.

During World War II I served with the 2nd Battalion, the
Royal Scots Fusiliers. Under a barrage from heavy guns,
arranged spectacularly – as always – by Field Marshall Sir
Bernard Law Montgomery (Monty to us), we moved north
from Sicily across the straits of Messina into the southern part
of Italy. Italian and German soldiers were in retreat. Our job
was to pursue them, remembering to search for stragglers in
every possible hiding place. Along the road we came to a
monastery which stood still and quiet on a green hillside, a
soap-bubble of apparent peace in the midst of the turmoil.

We had been without sleep for some time. We were mourning friends who had been killed in Sicily, my brother Archie
among them. We were tired and hungry and, I suppose, in the
coarse mood which becomes a kind of psychological armour
in time of war. (No, not a Christian mood, I agree.) We told the
fat cleric who seemed to be in charge that we should like all the
inmates to parade in the front yard so that the interior could be
searched without interference. In a short time the monks
began to come out.

They came out in incredible numbers, like gangsters emerging from a comic taxi in a Charlie Chaplin film. All wore tatty
brown robes with cowls. The majority were young men, all of
whom badly needed a shave. They were dirty, unkempt. Their
eyes were shifty. They smelt of incense and sweat.

Sergeant Hibbett, beside me, muttered in my ear: 'Holy
men, did you say, sir?'

'That's right. Though I should think most of them only
became holy when the war started.'

'It's enough to put you off religion,' he said.

I expect that among that parade were a few saintly men,
standing shoulder to shoulder with a number of recent deser-
ters from the Italian and German armies. But I made no effort
to hold a proper investigation. That could be done by the
Intelligence people behind us. We found nothing suspicious
inside and passed on. But I had difficulty in restraining my
fusiliers from kicking the bottoms of some of the younger
monks as they filed inside again, through the cloisters.

*   *   *

In the Middle Ages the Church was a great supranational authority, headed by the Pope, the Church in Scotland being a tiny part of it.

The trouble about such a set-up was that the Church tended to take advantage of its power and become dictatorial. And political affairs inevitably took a prominent place among its interests. Such political interests were not necessarily those of the people of the various countries which came under its control.

All this, of course, was nothing new. In prehistoric times the priestly scholars had raised stone monuments to celebrate their power. St Augustine had written a book called *The City of God* which claimed that the Church should rule over kings and nations. His idea was a good one and might have achieved some success had the Church continued to emphasize the simple lesson taught by Christ and resisted the temptation to assume material rather than spiritual power.

The people of medieval Scotland found their independence continually under threat not only by England, which wanted to make them subservient to English secular rule, but also by the Roman Church, which wanted to make them subservient to Roman spiritual rule and, in pursuance of that end, gave support to the English in their efforts to conquer Scotland.

The Church in Scotland, I am glad to say, though thirled to notions of holiness not altogether in tune with the Scottish character, was inclined to rebel against such dictatorship. It had some appreciation of the needs and desires of the people and had begun to provide encouragement for education. It founded schools, trained teachers and even then was formulating ideas which eventually led to the foundation of the great universities at St Andrews, Glasgow and Aberdeen. It gave some thought to the poor and established hospitals: hospitals sorely needed in a country suffering much from disease and continual war.

Scotland was in a turbulent situation similar to that of the Lebanon in recent times: under attack by an enemy without and torn within by fighting amongst various tribal and racial groups. But William Wallace, Paisley-born son of Sir Malcolm Wallace, chief vassal of the Steward of Scotland, dared to oppose the English (using their own brutal methods, let it be said) and, after winning the Battle of Stirling Bridge (1297), gave Scotland the chance to unite as an independent nation.

While most of the small landowners, tenant farmers, merchants and peasants gave him practical help, the 'aristocracy', anxious about their feudal interests in England, stood on the sidelines and made little effort to support him. He ruled with some success, however, restoring to Scots much land that had previously been held by Englishmen and initiating new trade links with the Hanseatic towns of Hamburg and Lubeck, reminding them that the Scots had now been 'recovered by war from the power of the English'.

But the 'recovery' lasted scarcely a year. Edward I, incensed by the turn events had taken, invaded Scotland again. Another battle was fought, this time at Falkirk (1298), in which heavy casualties were inflicted upon Wallace's army. William himself survived the battle, but his power in Scotland was undermined, especially in the south, where the strongholds of Bothwell, Roxburgh and Caerlaverock were destroyed by English soldiers.

In 1304 Edward besieged and won Stirling, 'the Cockpit of Scotland' and once again claimed all the lands north of Hadrian's Wall as part of England. Wallace was captured and taken to London, where, in 1305, he was hanged, drawn and emasculated. His head was cut off and displayed above London Bridge. His dismembered arms and legs were sent to Newcastle, Berwick, Perth and Aberdeen as an example to all 'rebels'.

Today, in Britain, with its sophisticated, 'civilized' society, such terrible killings are looked upon with horror. Not much horror is expressed, however, when political parties, aided and abetted by sections of the media, indulge in cruel character killings. Instead of axe-men and pikemen we have party chairmen and PROs. From a Christian standpoint is there a moral difference? Where is there even a hint of 'love thy neighbour'?

The Church in Rome made no comment on the medieval atrocities; but it maintained pressure on the Scottish Church to submit itself fully to England. The Scottish Church made no comment either, but within it there began to sprout again the seeds of a rebellion which had lain dormant since the Synod of

Whitby and the rule of Queen Margaret. A poor and spindly growth, perhaps, but it was there.

But if spiritual rebellion was fragile, physical rebellion burgeoned again when Robert the Bruce, Sheriff of Lanark in the service of England, came upon the scene. Though of Norman descent, Bruce believed he had a right to the crown of Scotland: a much better right, for example, than John Baliol, who had assumed it, but who now, beaten down in spirit by the aggression of Edward I, had retired to his estates in France, 'a broken, forgotten failure'; and a much better right than any member of the Comyn family, who were also claimants to the throne. He found enthusiastic allies in the Bishop of St Andrews and a number of lesser clergymen.

In an effort to bring about some kind of reconciliation a meeting was arranged between Bruce and the Comyns in a church at Dumfries. Almost immediately a quarrel broke out. Bruce took up his battle-axe and — perhaps by accident, it has been suggested — killed the Red Comyn.

Soon afterwards, on 25 March 1306, seated on the Stone of Destiny at Scone, and in the presence of the Abbots, he was crowned Robert I, King of Scotland, by Isabella, Countess of Buchan, whose family, the Earls of Fife, claimed a traditional right to perform the ceremony.

Edward I took a jaundiced view of such unilateral behaviour. He petitioned the Pope to sanction the destruction of Scone Abbey. The Pope, learning that the spiritual hierarchy in Scotland was becoming as rebellious as its secular leaders, gave Edward *carte blanche* to wage a punitive campaign.

The punishment was savage. Scone Abbey and other churches were razed to the ground. Three of Bruce's brothers were executed. His wife and the Countess of Buchan were imprisoned. The Scottish army was defeated by the English at Methven in Perthshire, and Bruce himself was forced to take refuge in remote parts of the west coast.

Such as Kintyre. Such as Southend at the Mull of Kintyre.

As I write this I can look out of my window and see, across the bay, the ruins of an ancient castle on Dunaverty Rock. It belonged to the MacDonalds, the Lords of the Isles, who, as Celts, never had much love for the Anglo-Saxons. For some time, while plotting his next moves, Bruce found Dunaverty a safe and hospitable place. His host was Aonghas Og (Young Angus) MacDonald, who had always been his friend.

Often, when words will not sing for me, when my bank statement is chilling and a strong wind from the sea is full of the rain and spray which make golf impossible, I climb the rock and stand among the ruins where Bruce once stood. He had been in a much worse plight than I, but despair had never come to him. Thinking about it all I feel better, a more confident member of the human race.

Because I remember, too, that Bruce's luck soon turned. Edward I died, leaving England under the rule of Edward II, an immature young fop whose knowledge of Scotland – and, indeed, his interest in it – was meagre. Bruce returned to the mainland of Scotland and found himself once again in command of a growing Scottish army: an army consisting not only of the nobility and their retinues but also of peasants and priests, merchants and tradesmen.

On the morning of 24 June 1314, 7000 Scots inspired by a common desire for freedom took up position at Bannockburn, on flat ground below the rugged height on which stood – and still stands – the strategically important Castle of Stirling. Behind them the dark mountains of their homeland. In front, 25,000 feudal mercenaries of the King of England, their 'banners right fairly flaming, their pencels in the wind waving'.

For me a story then unfolds in a way which may not appeal to unromantic historians. But all the facts are documented.

Before the battle the Scots knelt down while a passage from the bible was read by the Abbot of Inchaffray: 'Comfort ye, comfort ye, my people.' Then they listened to his prayer: 'Deliver us, O Lord from our enemies and from the hands of those that hate us.'

From the low ground Edward II saw them on their knees. He laughed. 'They are afraid! Will such men fight?' But his adherent, the Earl of Angus, though a quisling Scot, knew his countrymen. He shook his head and answered: 'Your majesty, they will fight. Those men are not afraid.'

Suddenly the Scots attacked: the men of Strathclyde and the Borders under Sir James Douglas; the men of Ross and Inverness under Thomas Randolph, Earl of Moray; the men of Buchan and Mar and Lennox under the king's brother,

Edward Bruce. Bruce himself commanded the reserve, made up of his own tenantry from Carrick and the clansmen from Argyll and the Isles.

The English were trapped between the rising waters of the Forth and the Bannock burn, so that their superior strength could not be deployed; and the battle swung decisively when Bruce, reinforcing success as Monty did more than 600 years later, called upon his friend Aonghas Og, MacDonald of the Isles, to rally his men and charge the English flank. 'My hope is constant in thee,' he said, words that can still be found on the Clanranald coat of arms.

Finally the *coup de grâce* was delivered by Bruce's own 'small folk', the farmers, the fishermen, the clerks and the weavers, the ordinary people for whose liberties Bruce was fighting.

For once all Scotland was united. Internal feuds among the nobility and quarrels among the tribal clans were, for the moment, forgotten. The Church, defying not only England but also Rome, was at one with the laity in a fervour of patriotism. The priestly scholars were now seeking power for the people rather than for themselves. In the years and centuries that followed the Scottish Kirk has never again completely abandoned the cause of freedom which it championed at the time of Bannockburn.

In his *History of the Church of Scotland* Dr R.R. MacEwan writes: 'In the case of every country which has had to contend for its freedom or independence, the relation between religion and patriotism has been important and has regulated the place of the Church in the affections and aspirations of the nation. In the case of Scotland, that relation at this stage of history was unique. Churchmen were on one side and the Church [of Rome] was on the other. The priesthood which derived its authority from Rome and was equipped with the Roman sacraments defied the authority and did not blanch before the full-voiced maledictions of the Roman Church.'

Seven years after Bannockburn, in 1320, the clergymen and laymen of Scotland sent a remarkable letter to the Pope. It is now called the Arbroath Declaration.

The passage from it most quoted runs as follows: 'While there exist a hundred of us we will never submit to England.

We fight not for glory, wealth or honour but for that liberty without which no virtuous man shall survive.'

But there is another passage which for me is equally important: 'Should he [the Bruce] abandon our cause or aim at reducing us or our kingdom, we will instantly expel him as our common enemy, and, under God, choose another King.'

It is hard to believe that such words were written while Robert I was at the height of his power and popularity. I look upon them as the faint, infant cries of a democracy which, in the years to come, was to transform the Scottish Kirk and nation.

9
'The Vices of the Age'

When Scots win national victories their pride becomes a euphoric fantasy experienced by all sections of the community, including the Kirk. Unity is all. Then internal jealousies and the echoes of old feuds lead to arguments. Adversaries busily twist knives in the cracks. National defeats become inevitable.

When such defeats occur the Scots are wracked by gloom, depression and bitterness. Pragmatic Anglo-Saxons often find this characteristic of ours difficult to understand.

Scotland's 'togetherness' after Bannockburn was soon at risk. The gap which had closed between the people on the one hand and the rulers and the priestly scholars on the other widened again.

The kings, lusting for money and power, encouraged the nobles to raid and harry the English. The nobles, lusting for power and land, demanded more and more of both for their services. The English, lusting for money and revenge, initiated attack after attack on Scotland. The tragedy of Flodden Field (1513), when 10,000 Scots were killed by the English under Thomas Howard, Earl of Surrey, loomed dark upon the horizon.

(Thomas Howard was an ancestor of the present Duke of Norfolk. The Norfolk coast of arms shows the top half of the Scottish lion with an arrow in its throat.)

Scottish churchmen seeking for peace and love through unity found their vision distorted by the greedy actions of their secular rulers (and patrons) and became greedy themselves. They found, too, that the people were beginning to be less and less satisfied with ornate religious ceremonies, pictures and images. They were completely uninterested in high-falutin' doctrinal arguments – of the 'How many angels can dance on the point of a pin?' variety – which had their genesis in the leisured palaces of popes and cardinals.

The shouts of triumph and pride at Bannockburn, dramatically echoed later by Burns in *Scots Wha Hae*, slowly stuttered down the scale into the whimpering cries of sadness and despair described in another famous song.

> I've heard the lilting at our yowe milking,
>   Lasses a-lilting before the dawn of day;
> But now they are moaning on ilka green loaning:
>   'The Flowers of the Forest are a' wede away.'

The Flowers of the Forest was written by Jean Elliot (1727– 1803), a daughter of Sir Gilbert Elliot, second baronet of Minto. Its opening line and the refrain – 'The Flowers of the Forest are a' wede (withered) away' – are traditional, as is the tune to which it is sung. Almost certainly they date from the time of Flodden. It has been suggested that 'the flowers of the forest' refer to James IV and his gallant company of young knights killed in the battle; but I believe that the song is also a lament for the harmony of country life so cruelly shattered by wars and preparations for wars and by the diseases, both physical and spiritual, which always follow in the wake of violence.

Before and after Flodden far-reaching social changes were taking place. Towns like Edinburgh, Glasgow and Aberdeen were growing. Merchants were finding new opportunities for trade in the alliance with France and in the aftermath of the exciting geographical discoveries by Columbus and Vasco da Gama. With the invention of gunpowder, knights in armour lost their glamour and widening cracks appeared in the Scottish feudal system.

Printing was invented and people began to read books. Becoming more self-conscious, individuals now ventured to believe that they might find Christ without the help of priests, without entering a monastery, without obeying fearful laws laid down by Rome. English translations of the New Testament enabled people to comprehend for themselves its simple message: a message that in the years and centuries following

Columba has become overlaid and obscured by clouds of legal and doctrinal practices.

In this 'seething cauldron of violence and social change' the Church in Scotland, as was only to be expected, became less well ordered and less prosperous. What ordinary folk wanted from it – what they have always wanted from it – was a promise of love and care and peace in a troubled world. Inhibited by secular pressures and, in some respects, losing heart and confidence, it was failing to deliver that promise.

Recovering from the shock administered to it by the Arbroath Declaration, Rome had again gathered to itself the reins of Church government in Scotland. In this it had the enthusiastic help of the English who took advantage of the premature deaths of several young and ineffective Scottish kings (deaths all connected with the continual struggle against England) and did their best to increase the weight of Roman Church law on the Scottish people – monarchs and nobles, merchants and tradesmen, priests and peasants all included.

And a real top-heavy weight it was.

In England the system of tithes had been introduced: a system in which landowners, merchants and farmers were supposed to contribute one-tenth of all their produce towards the maintenance of the parish priests. A similar system operated in Scotland, where tithes were called tiends. But Scottish priests were unlucky. During the sixteenth century most of the tiends were used to maintain the glory of the great cathedrals and abbeys and the high and mighty clergymen in charge of them.

That is, the cathedrals and abbeys left standing.

Since 1390 Elgin Cathedral had been in ruins, burned down by a royal prince during a quarrel with the church. In 1545 the abbeys of Kelso, Jedburgh, Melrose and Dryburgh were destroyed by the English. Newbattle Abbey was in a poor state, having been set on fire in 1385, like Melrose and Dryburgh, by rampaging English troops.

The parish priests were poorly paid, some earning only about £14 a year when professional men could expect up to £100. As a result the majority were poor in talent and poor in spirit. Many could not even write.

The late James Scotland, a favourite playwright among

modern amateur drama groups, wrote a series of comedies about Scottish church life in the fifteenth century. My amateur drama club, the Dunaverty Players of Southend, once reached the Final of the Scottish Community Drama Association's annual One Act Festival with *Hallowe'en*, which I believe is the best of them: it is certainly the most hilarious. And the ignorance and uninhibited sex life of James's cavorting and conniving monks and priests may not be too greatly exaggerated.

It is on record that monks at Inchcolm in Fife had what a modern gossip columnist might describe as 'living-in ladies'. St Columba would have been horrified to learn that over 800 years after his death one of the nuns in his beloved Iona was the daughter of a monk. Had that poor monkish father, cringing under the saint's thunderous rebuke, been gifted with foreknowledge he might have been tempted to reply: 'So what? Cardinal Beaton in St Andrews will have no less than eight illegitimate children, and Bishop Hepburn of Moray nine!'

'In the sixteenth century,' writes Tom Steele in *Scotland's Story*, 'two-fifths of all legitimations of bastards in Scotland were for the offspring of clergy.' Laymen, both educated and uneducated, were becoming critical of the Church. *Ane Satire of the Three Estates*, a cruel condemnation of its practices, was written and produced on the stage by Sir David Lyndsay. Years later, referring to Lyndsay, Sir Walter Scott wrote:

> The flash of that satiric rage,
> Which, bursting on the early stage,
> Branded the vices of the age
> And broke the keys of Rome.

Ane Satire of the Three Estates is still a popular choice of play at the Edinburgh Festival. Ministers of the present Church of Scotland swell the audiences. They are entertained and amused by it. But do I sometimes detect in their reactions an uneasy realization that it contains a warning?

And yet in medieval times Scotland had some religious leaders – both priests and poets – who bravely tried to uphold Christian standards.

James Kennedy, Bishop of St Andrews (died 1465), a descendant of the Bruce family, was a priestly scholar of wide learning, liberality and statesmanship. James II always took his advice when faced with problems concerning Church and State.

William Elphinstone, Bishop of Aberdeen, lived at the opening of the sixteenth century. James III and James IV both entrusted him with ambassadorial duties to foreign countries. He was aware that the people of Scotland longed for spiritual help from the Church, help which was not always available from a demoralized priesthood. He instituted special training for his clergy and, in 1494, founded King's College at Aberdeen.

This was at a time when the other Scottish universities then in existence – St Andrews, founded in 1411 and Glasgow founded in 1451 – were enrolling, almost exclusively, the teenage children of rich and powerful parents. By offering bursaries and other incentives, Elphinstone made sure that Aberdeen's doors were open to children of less wealthy parents and, indeed, to children of the poor.

He was also responsible for the publication of a service book – one of the earliest of Scottish printed works – now called the *Aberdeen Breviary*. He encouraged its distribution not only among the nobles, the landowners and their employees but also among the burgesses and ordinary citizens of the growing towns.

And, strange as it may seem, out of those chaotic times came some of the finest devotional poetry ever written in Scots, notably by Robert Henryson and William Dunbar.

Henryson offered succour and hope to his distraught and sorely confused contemporaries:

> Remember him that diet on tree,
> > For thy sake taistit the bitter gall
> Wha heis law hairtis, and lawis he:
> > Obey, and thank thy God of all.

In the spring of his youth Dunbar could write:

> Come, lustie summer! with thy flouris
> That I may lief in some disport.

In his old age, after long experience of what Neil Munro once described to me as 'the strange cantrips of the human heart', he could also write (in *The Merle and the Nightingale*):

All luf is lost bot upone God alone.

Despite the efforts of churchmen like Kennedy and Elphin-stone and of poets like Henryson and Dunbar, the general state of religious affairs in Scotland continued to deteriorate. Cor-ruption was rife. Abuses were many. There was capering in my Kirk more scandalous than had ever occurred before or has since.

The people were beginning to understand that in their unending search for love and peace not only the Scottish 'aristocracy' and their English counterparts but also the clergymen of the Scottish Church were offering abundant platitudes of law but a moiety of love. Could it be that they themselves ought now to take a more positive and forceful part in the government of the Church?

An idea bubbled and swelled. Again, as had happened more than once before – and as will happen again – flood-water began to press against a dam of repression and false propagan-da. Then it spilled over, turbulent and red like blood.

Its name was Reformation.

10
Justified by Faith?

The trouble about a bursting dam is that its flood-water is difficult to contain. It relieves dangerous pressures, but it also tends to spread destruction and sorrow along its path. The flood-water of the Reformation scoured out a jungle of corruption; but it did so at the expense of much human suffering in body and mind.

The Roman Church had built up a claim that it was omnipotent, the only medium of salvation for troubled souls. In the late fourteenth century a free-thinking Oxford don, by name John Wiclif, had challenged this claim. The Church, he said, was corrupted by wealth and superstition: he wanted it to return to the simple, straightforward ideals of the New Testament and to loosen the political and financial ties which often tethered it to the will of secular rulers.

A copy of Wiclif's translation of the Bible was brought to Scotland and parts of it translated into Scots. The message of God's love which it contained opened more and more eyes to the falsity of Rome's claim to supreme religious authority.

To stifle the suddenly audible cries for freedom of religious thought Rome and its secular supporters employed inhuman cruelty. John Huss, one of Wiclif's disciples, was burned to death in Prague in 1415. In Florence in 1495 Savonarola was also burned to death for preaching with power that the Roman Church required moral revival.

One influential critic did escape the physical lash of the Church's anger. He was a Dutchman, Erasmus, born *circa* 1466, the illegitimate son of a physician's daughter and a priest called Roger Gerard. He became an Augustinian canon at Steyn; but the monastic life was not to his humanistic taste and, in the outcome, he was given a Papal dispensation to return to the world and become a full-time writer.

His most important work was a scholarly translation of the Greek New Testament, to which he attached a prefatory essay. In this essay there are words which might have been written by St Columba:

'I could wish that every woman might read the Gospel and the Epistles of St Paul. Would that these were translated into each and every language so that they might be used and understood not only by Scots and Irishmen, but also by Turks and Saracens . . . Would that the farmer might sing snatches of Scripture at his plough, that the weaver might hum phrases of Scripture to the tune of the shuttle, that the traveller might lighten with stories from Scripture the weariness of the journey.'

Erasmus, like Columba, believed that Christianity should be practised not only in male-dominated Church observances but also in the ordinary lives of ordinary people, male and female at work and play.

One of his many published books was *Handbook for the Christian Soldier*, which concentrated people's minds on Christ's teachings rather than on the teachings of Popes and prelates and assorted 'saints'. He also wrote *Praise of Folly*, a scathing criticism of the churchmen of his time, the serial rights of which would be a magnet for the *Daily Mirror* of today. Or for *Private Eye*.

He died in Basel on 12 July 1536. His literary language was Latin; but his last words were spoken in his native Dutch: '*Lieve God*', 'Loving God'.

Erasmus's influence for reform was vigorous; but an even greater splintering of the dam occurred on 31 October 1517, when Martin Luther (1483–1546) nailed up on a church door in Wittenberg in Germany his *Theses*, which denounced a long list of abuses in the Church.

Luther was an Augustinian monk of powerful character, a priestly scholar whose study of the Bible had led him to the conclusion that *his* religious authority could only be God through Christ, and not the Pope through his politically minded cardinals and bishops. Christianity was paramount, not the Church. He believed in the Priesthood of all Believers and preached Justification by Faith. 'If a Christian has faith,' he said, 'he has everything. Faith unites Man to God.'

John Calvin (1507–64) was also a strong personality; but his character had none of the charisma evident in Luther's. Reserved, cold in manner, a stern Puritan, he was a writer trained in logic and the law, not an orator inspired by passion.

In Geneva he set up a system of reformed doctrine, worship and discipline which became the model not only for the Protestantism of Scotland but also for that in Holland, France, Hungary, America and elsewhere. His *Institutes of the Christian Religion*, first published in 1536, enlarged upon his firm adherence to the doctrine of the Sovereignty of God. And yet, despite his hard-line reputation, Calvin did have a human side. Advocates in Scotland of Sabbaths 'black and bleak' are probably unaware that their august exemplar often enjoyed a game of bowls on a Sunday. Luther, they should also be reminded, was not averse to a dram or two at his regular Sunday-night parties.

Erasmus, Luther, Calvin: they may have been heretical in the eyes of the Church, but it was becoming apparent that many people – and even some rulers – had sympathy for their cause. The idea of democracy was beginning to oust that of dictatorship. Education had caused people to realize that if divinity could exist in kings and priestly scholars it could also exist in themselves as fellow human beings. Therefore they had as much right to their opinions as those set up in authority over them. We need authority in Church and State, they might have said, otherwise life would be even more chaotic than it is; but such an authority ought to exist for the benefit of all, not just for the benefit of those who wield it. For this reason it must be an authority chosen not by kings or priestly scholars but by everybody.

Such ideas burgeoned in Scotland rather more slowly than in the rest of Europe. So did the Reformation of the Church. This was partly because of the savage treatment suffered by some of those who advocated it. (Such treatment, savage though it was, did not reach the horrendous scale of, for example, the Spanish Inquisition.)

John Resby, a rebellious English priest, was burned to death in Perth in 1406. Paul Crawer, who tried to disseminate the teachings of John Huss, Wiclif's disciple, was burned to death at St Andrews in 1433. In 1494 some thirty people known as the Lollards of Kyle were charged with Wiclif 'heresies'.

In Southend few memories remain of that morally and physically tortured age. But there is a story, hinted at in modern ordnance survey maps, which may provide evidence of what was happening even in such a remote corner of the kingdom as Kintyre.

On the coast, two and a half miles north of the lighthouse at the Mull, there is a derelict farm called *Innean Coig Cailleiche*, 'the *innean* of the five old women'. (An *innean* in Kintyre signifies a grassy area above the shore bounded by steep, rock-strewn slopes in the form of an amphitheatre.) Included in the farmland is a cemetery, long disused, in which at least forty graves have been counted. It is probably a burying-place created by the inhabitants of the numerous small farms which once existed at or near the Mull when the population of the parish was six times greater than it is today.

The story goes that the 'five old women' were nuns, expelled from a monastery or cell called *Caibel Carrine* (St Catharine's Chapel), the remains of which can still be seen on the west bank of the Breckrie near Low Glenadale House. It appears that the reason for their expulsion, by angry neighbours, was loose living, superstitious practices and neglect of their religious duties.

If the story is true, then the flood-water of the Reformation was bubbling in Southend as far back as 1481, when 'Enynookalach' is first mentioned in parish records.

A small spring bubbles into a well beside the ruins of *Caibel Carrine*. The water is supposed to have valuable medicinal properties, and it is customary for anyone drinking it to tie a rag containing a piece of money to the lower branches of the surrounding trees. Rags still flutter from branches overhanging the well, evidence that visitors are unwilling to flout an ancient custom; but I have yet to discover any money enclosed in their folds.

Perhaps pagan superstition is indeed dying out under the influence of Christianity, though even with the help of Erasmus, Luther, Calvin and the rest it is taking a long, long time. Or is the absence of money in the newly tied cloths simply the result of miserly monetarism, that more up-to-date but equally unloving superstition?

It was the fate of Patrick Hamilton (1503–28) which finally breached the parapet of the religious dam in Scotland.

Hamilton was an 'aristocrat', a great-grandson of James II. His appointment as Abbot of Fearn in Ross-shire, while still a boy and incapable of carrying out any spiritual duties, is an example of how, at the time, the Church's money was often spent, not on the work of priests in the parishes but on what we might call jobs for the privileged.

But as he grew up Patrick began to take his duties seriously. At the age of fifteen, after a spell in Paris as a student, he went on to study under Erasmus at Louvain. Later, while attending a theological course at the reformed University of Marburg in Germany, he wrote *Patrick's Places*, which demonstrated clearly the need for reformation in the Church. Such a stodgy title would find favour with few publishers today, if I judge them aright. Nevertheless, the book became a best-seller.

Returning to Scotland – to Linlithgow – he began to preach Christianity in the Lutheran word. 'Thou must do good works,' he said, 'but beware that thou do them not to deserve any good through them.' To the hierarchy of the Church in Scotland, cocooned in wealth and privilege, this was a dangerous line of thought. Archbishop David Beaton, feigning friendly interest, invited Patrick to St Andrews to expound his views. Eagerly the young man accepted the challenge; but by doing so he supplied all the evidence against him that Beaton wanted. On 28 February 1528 he was tried, condemned as a heretic and burned at the stake in front of St Salvator's College.

It was raining that day. The bonfire smouldered and smoked and Hamilton took six hours to die. At an early stage, while onlookers pled with him to recant and save his life, he told them: 'As to my confession I will not deny it for awe of your fire, for my confession and belief is in Jesus Christ.'

He was only twenty-five years old when he died. But his death ensured that Reformation would flow as strongly in Scotland as it had already done in England and on the

Continent. As was said at the time, 'The reek of Master Hamilton has infected as many as it blew upon.'

It may have infected another Reformer, a tall, dark-haired, long-bearded schoolmaster called George Wishart (1512–46), described as 'courteous in manner, simple in his way of living, very charitable, an earnest teacher'. After studying in Switzerland and Germany he came back to preach Reform in Scotland, notably in Dundee. In order to further his religious cause he also became a political activist, an agent of English Protestantism under Henry VIII.

Archbishop Beaton saw him at once as a threat to the Franco-Scottish Alliance which, in Church as well as State, now regarded England as its bitter enemy. He had Wishart arrested and, like Patrick Hamilton, burned to death at St Andrews.

Wishart's 'minder', who often accompanied him on perilous preaching tours carrying a two-handed sword, was a Haddington man called John Knox. On the night of his arrest Wishart sent Knox away. 'One of us,' he said sombrely, 'is sufficient for a sacrifice.'

As always happens, such violence bred more violence. In the early morning of 29 May 1546 a group of Fife Protestants, led by William Kirkcaldy of Grange, broke into the Archbishop's castle and hung him, dying, from the window at which he had watched Wishart burn. It was a Reformer who wrote:

> Although the loon was well away
> The deed was foully done.

Kirkcaldy, it is said, had been recruited as an agent by Henry VIII, that great champion, on the surface, of Protestantism. Henry had no qualms about using religion as a political tool. He had learned that he could do so with impunity when the Pope refused him a divorce from the Queen, Catherine of Aragon, and he set himself up as a kind of secular Pope in England.

Such barbaric killings in the name of religion, could they occur today in our 'enlightened', 'civilized' society? The answer is more bitter than a lemon. It could, at the end of the day, be a nuclear bomb.

Because flood-waters are building up again.

Two world wars have been waged, both sides, on each occasion, claiming the blessing of God. Hitler killed thousands of Jews with a cold savagery which would have shocked even his forebear, Attila the Hun. Stalin eliminated countless 'rebels', some of whom, in the name of Christ, dared to oppose his dictatorship. Truman destroyed thousands of innocent lives in a nuclear holocaust staged in Japan.

In the Lebanon Christians slaughter Jews and Moslems, Moslems slaughter Jews and Christians, Jews slaughter Christians and Moslems without discrimination. In Northern Ireland Roman Catholics kill Protestants and Protestants kill Roman Catholics in a frenzy of political hatred. In South Africa white people who claim to be Christians and boast a spiritual affinity with Luther and Calvin do not hesitate to torture, shoot and hang their political opponents. Black people retaliate with equal savagery.

Revolutionary movements throughout the centuries – movements great and small – may have brought faith and hope; but they have always failed to deliver the love longed for by ordinary people. Will future revolutions contain the ingredient of charity as well as the faith and the hope?

If not, then the answer is bound to be a nuclear bomb. And curtains for humankind.

11
'First ae caper, syne anither'

John Knox, having taken Wishart's advice to escape Beaton's anger, made the most of his opportunity. The death of his mentor had curious echoes of the death of Christ: perhaps this was what inspired him as a dour fighter for religious freedom. If Peter was the rock upon which the universal Church was founded, it may be argued that Knox was the rock upon which the Presbyterian Church of Scotland was founded.

His personal struggle to establish the Reformation in Scotland, faced as he was by many religious and political handicaps, reads like a film treatment.

As Scotland's ally, France did all in her power to save her for Rome; and for a time it seemed as if Scotland might be turned into a French dependency, both in Church and State.

On one of their expeditions the French fleet raided St Andrews and captured Knox, who, after Beaton's hanging, had become chaplain to the garrison there. For seventeen months he worked as a slave in a French warship.

He himself has told the story of how one day, as he and his fellow slaves slumped, resting, upon their oars, a priest came down the central platform of the ship showing an image of the Virgin Mary to each man for his comfort and adoration. When it came to Knox's turn he snatched the image from the priest and hurled it into the sea, shouting out that it was an idol, a mere 'painted bredd' (piece of wood). (If the story is true, I cannot imagine how he escaped dire punishment.)

On another occasion, as the galley was patrolling the Scottish coast, Knox said that he glimpsed the steeple of Holy Trinity Church, St Andrews, where he had preached his first sermon. He made a vow to himself that he would preach there again in better times. He did, too.

Peace with France ultimately gave Knox his release. He was sent back to England where, encouraged by Edward VI and Cranmer, Protestantism was now a swelling surge. He was made a king's chaplain and, for a time, conducted a successful ministry in Berwick. This was as near as he could get to his beloved Scotland, still in 'religious' turmoil, still a dangerous place for an outspoken Reformer.

In 1533 Mary succeeded her half-brother Edward VI on the English throne. She was a fervent supporter of the Roman Church, and Knox – and many others – thought it expedient to leave the country. He went to Switzerland and there, while he ministered to the English congregation in Geneva, he met Calvin, for whose religious teachings he conceived a profound admiration.

Meanwhile, in Scotland Mary of Guise had for some time been acting as regent for her young daughter, Mary Queen of Scots. She was strong for the Roman Church and used French troops to counter the growing threat of Protestantism. The people, always dourly independent, had been keen enough to accept France as an ally against England. Now they realized that France was aiming to be more than an ally: she was on the verge of becoming their dictatorial ruler. In consequence they turned for moral and practical aid to their old antagonists, the English, enemies of France and Protestant as well.

In 1557 five noblemen calling themselves the 'Lords of the Congregation' made a covenant to renounce the Roman Church and strive against Mary of Guise to make Scotland Protestant. During the following year they were encouraged in their efforts when on Mary Tudor's death Elizabeth became Queen of England and began, with some energy, to oppose Roman Catholics. From her they were promised military assistance. Then, to strengthen their cause still further, they summoned John Knox home.

Knox found Scotland in a state next to civil war: supporters of the Crown and the Roman Church versus the revolutionary, independence-seeking Protestants.

In general the public were on the side of the revolution, not only because they had been sickened by the low morals of those who called themselves 'religious' but also because they wanted rid of French influence. The nobility were divided.

Some supported the Crown for 'religious' reasons, others because they feared losing their power in the land. Some supported the Protestants for 'religious' reasons, others because they calculated that the new movement might enrich them with land which had belonged to the Church.

It was all a wild mixture of hot emotion and cold self-interest, and Christianity only flickered weakly in the hearts and minds of a few.

> Ev'n Satan glower'd and fidg'd fu' fain,
> An' hotched an' blew wi' might an' main:
> Till first ae caper, syne anither,
> Tam tint his reason a' thegither.

But Knox did not lose his reason. With passionate conviction he turned the swirling flood-water into a straight channel: a channel that was religious rather than political and social.

In St Andrews and Edinburgh he preached the gospel of Christ in plain Scots, a language that ordinary folk could understand, assuring all sinners that salvation did not come from the patronage of priestly scholars intoning prayers in Latin but by the sincere faith within a man's own heart. His oratory fired the blood. An English listener wrote: 'The voice of that one man was able to put more life in us in one hour than five hundred trumpets blustering in our ears.'

But, as the 'Lords of the Congregation' had shrewdly reckoned, in a political sense Knox could also be a rabble-rouser. On 11 May 1559 he preached a famous sermon in St John's Church in Perth, denouncing what he called 'idolatry' in the Roman Church. While he spoke a priest approached the altar to say Mass. A teenage boy threw a stone at him. The congregation rioted. Images were pulled down, sacred pictures torn to pieces. The mob stormed outside. An abbey and two monasteries in the town were attacked and stripped of their precious ornaments, their linen and furniture, their meat and wine, then set on fire.

The riot continued for two days. The mayhem spread to Scone, two miles away, where part of the abbey was destroyed. Flames and smoke rose high above the grey buildings and the 'Lords of the Congregation' rejoiced in the discomfiture of Mary of Guise. Had television reporters and cameramen existed at the time what splendid 'copy' they would have had, with politicians and churchmen offering every kind of reason for the rioting except the true one, which was that the people, seeking love and peace, were being denied both by those set in spiritual and material authority over them.

Made bolder by such evidence of public support, the 'Lords of the Congregation' assembled an army, occupied St Andrews and sacked the town's bright and beautiful cathedral. Mary of Guise and her French army were forced to retreat, first to Edinburgh, then to Dunbar, where they waited for help to come from France. But when troop reinforcements did arrive – 2000 of them – the Scottish army had been supplemented by English soldiers and an English fleet was setting up a blockade of the French garrison in Leith.

Apart from her support of the Protestant cause, Elizabeth of England had another more personal reason for helping the 'rebel' Scots. The French king had published propaganda to the effect that Elizabeth was illegitimate and that, therefore, his wife, Mary of Scots, was the rightful heir to the English throne through her descent from Henry VII. Elizabeth was determined to nip what she called 'this nonsense' in the bud. (Twenty-eight years later, in 1587, she finally rid herself of embarrassment when she had Mary beheaded.)

During the siege of Leith, Mary of Guise became ill with dropsy and died in Edinburgh Castle on 11 June 1560. French resistance collapsed. On 6 July 1560, by the Treaty of Edinburgh, the French agreed to withdraw all their troops from Scotland and to recognize Elizabeth as Queen of England. The Scots were not party to the Treaty; but the 'Lords of the Congregation' saw to it that concessions were made to them. In future no foreigners would be appointed to office in Scotland. The government of the country would be entrusted to a council of twelve, seven nominated by Mary the Queen (who was still in France) and five by the Scottish Parliament.

Mary, now widowed, returned from France in 1561 to occupy the throne of Scotland. John Knox worked hard to establish the Protestant advantage in what was still, on paper, a Roman Catholic country. Many of the nobility gave him little help, because they suspected that the creation of a new Church would cost them money and put them out of favour

with the Queen, who was passionately for Rome. But the
Scottish Parliament, with a majority of the middle-class gentry
in favour of political independence from France, England and
Rome, was on his side.

In August 1560 it officially abolished the jurisdiction of the
Pope in Scotland. It also rejected the Episcopal system as
practised by the Church in England and approved a *Confession of Faith* which Knox and a committee of five other
ministers had put together in the space of less than a week.

Oddly enough, those five ministers had the same Christian
name as their chairman. They were John Row, John Spottis-
woode, John Winram, John Douglas and John Willock.

The Scots Confession, 'wholesome and sound doctrine
grounded upon the infallible truth of God's word', had the
Bible as its foundation rock. Everybody, rank and status in
society immaterial, would share in the Sacrament of the Lord's
Supper. Thus God would come to a congregation not so much
through 'idolatrous' bread and wine as through people wor-
shipping in loving communion with one another. The Church
was the people and at communion the people themselves
became the body of Christ. It was a concept springing Christian fresh in a garden choked with doctrinal weeds.

But it was not a new concept. It was the rebirth of one
expressed in a poem said to have been written by St Patrick in
Ireland 1100 years earlier; a poem often quoted by St Columba.

> Christ with me, Christ before me.
> Christ behind me, Christ within me.
> Christ in the heart of everyone who thinks of me,
> Christ in the mouth of everyone who speaks to me,
> Christ in every eye that sees me,
> Christ in every ear that hears me.

The Scots Confession has been described as 'the warm
utterance of a people's heart'. At the time it was criticized by
some as promulgating new and unauthorized religious beliefs;
but Knox and his supporters insisted that, on the contrary, it
stood for the pure Christian faith of the Church, the simple,
unadulterated, Biblical faith once delivered to the saints of old:
a faith clear and unambiguous as compared with Romanism

which, over the centuries, had become 'corrupt, obscured and confused'.

When the beadle – or in these less prosperous days, the duty elder – carries in the big Bible at the beginning of a service and lays it reverently on pulpit board or lectern, he or she is drawing attention to the claim that Scottish Prebyterianism stems directly from its pages.

The Knox Committee, as no doubt it would be called today, also produced a *Book of Discipline*. This proposed many of the ideas which give basic strength to the Church of Scotland as it is now constituted. The most revolutionary, perhaps, was one which insisted that certain laymen, to be called elders, should be given responsibility in religious matters. Furthermore, each parish was to appoint a Kirk Session consisting of elders to help the minister. And there was to be a General Assembly, attended by laymen as well as clergymen.

The Committee went on to suggest other changes. Ministers should have manses and glebes and receive payments comparable to those of other professional people. Sons of the manse were to be eligible for bursaries so that they could attend universities. Ministers' widows were to be generously provided for. There should be relief for the poor and, of paramount importance, a national system of free, compulsory education: 'a school in every parish', as advocated by John Knox himself.

The rich and powerful nobles in Parliament, listening to all this, suddenly realized that as the principal donors of tiends they would be required to contribute a great deal of money if such schemes were to be implemented. They also suspected that if the Church became the vigorous and well-endowed entity of Knox's imagination it might prove a dangerous political threat. A majority of their number, greedily intent upon acquiring more lands, more money and more power for themselves – as their predecessors in prehistoric and medieval times had been and as their successors in modern times still are – refused to ratify the clauses which threatened their pockets and their status in society.

But, though the complete reorganization of the Church was still a matter of argument and strife, Scotland had now, at last, become officially Protestant. John Knox died in 1572, knowing that the deaths of the martyrs and his own hard, implacable battle against Rome had not been in vain. Scottish Presbyterianism had now a foot in the door.

English Episcopacy, however, was trying to shut it again.

12
An Anvil for Many Hammers

Reformation had come to Scotland, as it had come to Europe and England, on a flood of physical violence and political hypocrisy. In the years that followed, the Christian ideal of love still struggled to survive in the Church under a load of more violence and hypocrisy.

Little love was evident, for example, in the relationship between Mary, the Roman Catholic Queen, and Knox, the Protestant Reformer. Quite simply, they hated each other.

Mary hated Knox because he condemned the Church to which she was devoted and also because she believed him to be arrogant, uncouth in speech and entirely insensitive to her status as a woman: a woman moreover with, as she thought, a divine right as Queen to his obedience. Knox hated Mary because she so warmly supported the Roman Church and also because he believed her to be a dictatorial young lady of dubious morals, insensitive to the spiritual and physical needs of ordinary folk.

They screamed and shouted at each other, and the doves of peace were devoured by squabbling hawks.

But, though she tried hard enough, Mary did not devour Protestantism. It was a bird strong enough to survive all attacks, even the divisive humours within its own body. And, though he also tried hard enough, Knox did not devour Roman Catholicism. It survived — and still survives — in the hearts and minds of many Scots.

Knox died and Mary died: Knox in Edinburgh in the bosom of his family, Mary in England, far from home, her neck severed by an axe.

In his personal life Knox found hardship and tragedy but some happiness, too. His first wife, Marjory Bowes, died in

1560, leaving him two sons. In 1564, at the age of fifty-one, he married a girl of sixteen — Margaret Stewart, a daughter of Lord Ochiltree — by whom he had three daughters.

In her personal life Mary found nothing but tragedy. While still in her early twenties she had been forced, one way or another, to marry in quick succession three husbands: the young, sickly, physically crooked Francis, Dauphin of France; the violent, womanizing, morally crooked Darnley; and the criminally crooked, murdering rapist, Bothwell. When her head fell from the block, Simon Bulle, her executioner, snatched at its thick auburn hair in an attempt to hold it high. The hair came away in his hand, revealing grey, straggling wisps beneath the wig. Her death took place on 8 February 1587. She was only forty-four.

Meanwhile Protestantism was flooding throughout Scotland northwards from the Lowlands to the Highlands, and even out to the Western Isles where people still remained, by a majority, Roman Catholic. But following the failure of the Scottish Parliament to carry out all the recommendations suggested in the *First Book of Discipline*, bitter controversy arose as to how the Church in Scotland, now that it had broken free of Rome, should be organized and governed.

Nothing in the secular and religious history of Scotland is simple and straightforward as, perhaps laboriously, I have been endeavouring to show. This is because the Scots can always be roused to passionate but often illogical disputations amongst themselves, the only common ground of which is a vaguely perceived ideal of freedom and independence. Typically, therefore, the controversy in the post-Reformation Church had two intertwining roots. On the one hand it was a controversy between Protestant Presbyterian and Protestant Episcopalian systems of Church government. On the other hand, it was a controversy between the Stewart kings (always sib to Rome) and the General Assembly in Scotland as to which should rule the Church.

Scotland at the time was a neglected garden, with various plants and shrubs all seeking life and, in the process, strangling and killing one another. Christ, the head gardener, had issued clear instructions as to its proper cultivation, but a number of his local assistants were sitting in the greenhouse spending their energy not on actually doing the work but, instead, in arguing angrily as how they should proceed with it.

In the Presbyterian system all clergymen are of one rank. Those ordained to its ministry are charged with all its pastoral and administrative functions. There are some, of course, whose talents may be used for necessary superintendence and administration, but these remain of the same order as the parish ministers. (In the original New Testament Greek the word for 'minister' is 'presbyteros'.) In the Episcopalian system there are bishops, said to be the successors of the Apostles. They have vast authority over the 'ordinary' clergy, and certain functions of the pastoral ministry are reserved exclusively for them.

In Presbyterianism the government of the church is in the hands of the people, through their elected parish ministers and elders who meet together at appointed times in Sessions, Presbyteries, Synods and General Assembly. Though lay people do take part in it, Episcopalian Church government is in the main influenced by appointed, not elected, bishops. In straightforward terms (if, for once, as a Scot, I can persuade myself to think straightforwardly) the Presbyterian system is democratic, while the Episcopalian system is autocratic, not so far removed from the dictatorial Roman one.

Presbyterianism is Scottish. The Episcopalian system is English, its origins due to Henry VIII who, when becoming a Protestant for personal and political reasons, immediately assumed the leadership of the Church in place of the Pope.

The Stewart kings, beginning with James VI in Scotland, all believed in the divine right of kings to have absolute authority not only over the State but also over the Church. The idea was accepted without too much difficulty by the Episcopalians, who themselves were an autocratic order; but it was anathema to the Presbyterians.

The man who gave the most vivid expression to such anathema was Andrew Melville (born 1545) who, at various times, was a university lecturer at Geneva, the Principal of Glasgow University and the Principal of St Mary's College, St Andrews.

During his years at Geneva Melville came under the influence of Theodore Beza, a prominent disciple of Calvin and, in many eyes, his successor. Once, during an argument with his king, Beza uttered words which have become historic: 'Sire, it belongs in truth to the Church of God to endure blows and not to inflict them; but it will also please your majesty to remember that the Church is an anvil that has worn out many hammers.'

Returning to Scotland in 1574, Melville did much for Scottish education, especially in his efforts to discover and train efficient ministers. (Such effort ought to provide a salutary example to the Church of Scotland today.) He also became the champion of the Presbyterian cause in opposition to any form of Episcopacy. As Moderator of the General Assembly he complained loudly and angrily against interference with the Church by the civil authorities and composed the draft of a set of rules for Church government which would set it free from such interference. At one stage he led a deputation of ministers to explain these rules to the King and the King's Council.

'Who,' demanded one of the nobles in the Council, 'will subscribe to these treasonable articles?'

Melville stepped forward at once and took up a pen. 'We dare,' he said, 'and will subscribe and render our lives in the cause.'

In 1581, Melville persuaded the Church to accept a *Second Book of Discipline*, an enlarged and only slightly revised version of the *First Book of Discipline*.

It laid emphasis upon the importance of parish ministers and elders elected by the congregations. 'As the pastors should be diligent in teaching and sowing the Word, so the elders should be careful in seeking the fruits of the same among the people.' Deacons were also to be elected, particularly charged with the care of the poor. And, for the first time, the idea that ministers and elders from neighbouring parishes should meet regularly in 'presbyteries' was hinted at.

But, as far as antagonism to Episcopacy was concerned, the sting was in the tail. 'The civil power should command the spiritual to exercise and do their office concerning the Word of God. The spiritual rulers should require the Christian magistrate to minister justice and punish vice *and to maintain the liberty and quietness of the Kirk.*'

When James VI tried to argue about this, Melville told him: 'There are twa King's and twa kingdoms in Scotland; there is Christ Jesus and his kingdom the Kirk, whose subject King James the sixth is, and of whose kingdom, not a king, nor a lord, nor a head, but a member.'

Furious, the king persuaded Parliament to pass the so-called 'Black Acts' (1584) which reaffirmed Episcopal Church government in Scotland and ensured that the Church should be ruled not by a General Assembly but by bishops appointed by the king. This meant that the king, with his Parliament and Council, now claimed complete supremacy not only over the State but also over the Church.

For a time, fearful of his liberty and even of his life, Melville had to leave the country, accompanied by some of his followers.

But then King James, who had his ambition more firmly fixed upon being Elizabeth's successor on the throne of England than upon being head of the Scottish Church, began to have trouble with various nobles and men of influence whose aim was to restore a Roman Catholic monarchy. In the face of a new burgeoning threat from Rome, the king thought it politic to give grudging support to Melville's blue-print for Protestantism in Scotland.

In 1592, impelled by manifest unrest among the people, the Scottish Parliament, unhindered by James, acknowledged and ratified the system of Church government as outlined in the *Second Book of Discipline*. Several of the clauses from the *First Book of Discipline* which previously had been turned down were included. At last Melville had secured what has been called the Magna Carta of Scottish Presbyterianism.

It must be said, however, that the *Second Book of Discipline* contained some recommendations which smacked more of tyranny than of Christian charity.

For example, it was laid down that the Sabbath day should begin at six o'clock on a Saturday evening and last twenty-four hours, during which time no work was to be done. Nothing was to be bought or sold on a Sunday, alehouses were to be closed and music, dancing and gaming banned. Ministers of the Kirk were instructed to wear hodden-grey suits on weekdays and blue serge on a Sunday.

And the Church was empowered to administer dire punishment to proven – and sometimes unproven – transgressors. An instrument was invented, called the 'brank', an iron helmet with a triangular tongue which could be thrust into the 'sinner's' mouth to silence evil talk. 'Witches' and 'sorcerers' were liable to be tortured and burned at the stake. So were 'fornicators'.

It can be argued that here was the origin of the black and joyless reputation which still clings to the Church of Scotland in the insular journalistic hives of London, where Jean Rook is a Queen Bee. And, indeed, in one sense it was a rule of fear imposed by priestly scholars: a rule which echoes those probably current in Old Testament times and during the Romanism of the medieval period.

In the context of the bloody religious and political violence of the sixteenth and seventeenth centuries, however, there may have been some excuse for it as being a natural human reaction to worse evils. But the fires of Christian love still burned low.

Christian love burned low indeed in the tortuous, homosexual mind of King James. When in 1603 he achieved his ambition and became not only James VI of Scotland but also James I of England, he left Scotland and established his court in London. There he found that his divine right as ruler of Church and State was accepted without too much opposition. Encouraged by this he decided that Scotland should be brought into line and the Episcopalian system of Church government officially established throughout the whole country.

In 1606 Andrew Melville and seven other Scottish ministers were summoned to a conference in London. Melville snorted his objections to the king's idea and composed a Latin epigram which ridiculed an Episcopalian service held for his benefit in the Chapel Royal. For this 'insolence' to a divine monarch the English Privy Council sent him to the Tower, where he remained for five years, powerless to mount further opposition to the king's plans.

Eventually, through the intercession of the Duke of Bouillon, who wanted him as a professor in the University of Sedan, he was released. He died in Sedan in 1622, sadly aware that the condition of the Church in Scotland was still in angry flux.

In 1618, after much wheeling and dealing, the king persuaded the Scottish Church to accept the Five Articles of Perth. These included kneeling at Communion, permission to have Communion privately, permission to have private baptisms, confirmation by bishops and the strict observance of Christmas, Easter and other saints' days. But many Scots, fearful that James was making subtle moves towards a return to Romanism, voiced strong opposition.

They believed that the Pope was the Antichrist of the Book of Revelation and that Roman Catholicism was an anti-God movement. They were aware that in Europe the so-called Thirty Years' War had begun, which in its early stages was a fairly clean-cut struggle between Protestantism and Romanism: a struggle which Romanism looked like winning. They were aware also that the freedom of the Church would be gravely compromised if Episcopacy, which bowed to the wishes of the State, took root in Scotland.

'Feeling in Scotland,' writes Professor Henderson, 'grew stronger in favour of freedom for the Church to guide its own spiritual life, puritan simplicity of worship to avoid Romish superstition and to make sure of inward reality in approaching God, and the Presbyterian form of Church government to keep things out of the power of the State and give the people a share in the regulation of religious affairs.'

Behind it all was the strong trait in the Scottish character which resents and opposes any attempt to undermine its freedom of thought and action in religious, political and cultural affairs. When anybody seems to overlook the fact that we are a nation in our own right then the thistle stings. *Nemo me impune lacessit*.

When King James's son, Charles I, came to the throne in 1625 the pressure for Episcopacy in Scotland grew stronger. Scottish disquiet grew stronger, too. People feared to have 'our poor country made an English Province'. Advised by Laud, the Archbishop of Canterbury, but without consulting Scottish ministers, Charles ordered that the English Prayer Book, containing many echoes of Romanism, should be used in every pulpit in Scotland. He believed he had a duty to do so, as a king with divine right.

On 23 July 1637, in St Giles's Church in Edinburgh, the

minister attempted to read from the new Prayer Book. In the person of the famous Jenny Geddes the thistle stung. 'Wad ye say mass at my lug!' she screeched and flung her stool at him. Inevitably this caused a riot which, in its turn, engendered further riots. A conviction grew among the leaders of the Church and the nobles that the time had come to nullify Charles's attempts at absolute rule.

A National Covenant was drawn up to achieve this end. It was mainly the work of Alexander Henderson, minister at Leuchars in Fife, and Archibald Johnston of Wariston, a young lawyer who supported with fervour the Presbyterian cause. Their stated intention was 'to recover the purity and liberty of the Gospel' and to ensure 'that religion and right-eousness may flourish in the land to the Glory of God, the honour of the king, and peace and comfort to us all.'

The signing of the Covenant began in Greyfriars Kirk in Edinburgh on 28 February 1638. Copies of the document were distributed for signing by individuals and congregations, and diaries of the time record much religious and patriotic excite-ment throughout the country.

Some people signed the Covenant with their blood, loudly boasting their resolve to 'obey God rather than men'.

The General Assembly met in Glasgow Cathedral in November 1638, with the laity present in large and voluble numbers. Alexander Henderson was Moderator and Archi-bald Johnston the Clerk. The Marquis of Hamilton, represent-ing Charles I, endeavoured to stem the flood of opposition to the king. When he failed in this he declared the Assembly dissolved.

But the Assembly had the bit in its teeth. It ignored the marquis and continued in session. By large majorities it set aside the Episcopalian system of Church government, rejected all 'English' innovations in forms of worship and firmly re-established the place of elders in the courts of the Church. Passionate anger at what it believed to be Steward attempts to Romanize the Protestant Kirk resulted in some of the chief opponents of the Covenant being excommunicated. 'We have now,' said Alexander Henderson, 'cast down the walls of Jericho.'

The thistle flaunted its purple flowers.

13
Confession

John Buchan said, 'Without some understanding of the Church there can be no true understanding of Scottish history or the nature of the Scottish people.' As a student of all three, striving to follow the tortuous trails of truth, I am bound to agree with him, though I suspect that 'true understanding' frequently eludes me. Perhaps this is because I am a Scot myself, entangled among the trees and too close to them to see the wood.

The people of Scotland – like people everywhere – have always had a deep longing for love and peace. And liberty. But when we are deprived of these something in our character causes us to react with resentful anger, both spiritual and physical, rather than with argument and example, as is the Christian way. In modern times I believe that in the Church at least we are recapturing Christ's message – the message of 'love thy neighbour', no matter what – though political trees in the wood still cast confusing shadows and, again characteristically, we squabble among ourselves as to the best way out into the sunlight.

At the General Assembly of 1638 Scotland's desire for the spiritual freedom of Protestantism and Presbyterianism was firmly stated. England also desired spiritual freedom and Protestant democracy. When Charles I, by force of arms, tried to assert his divine right as an omnipotent ruler, the English Parliament drew up in 1643 a Solemn League and Covenant – not to be confused with the Scottish National Covenant of 1638 – which undertook to extirpate 'Popery and Prelacy'. It involved a treaty with the Scottish Church, signed in Edinburgh, promising mutual help against a dictatorial king. The outcome was a civil war, often described in the headline language to which we have become more and more accustomed as Roundheads versus Cavaliers. And Cromwell, in order to displace a dictator, became a dictator himself: a phenomenon which occurs regularly today in countries all over the world.

A Scottish army was dispatched to fight in England on Cromwell's side and took part in the decisive battle of Naseby in 1643. It was to the Scots that King Charles surrendered; but under pressure they handed him over to their English allies, who executed him in 1646.

During this period of puritan revolution a great assembly took place at Westminster. It was attended by a few Scottish ministers and elders who hoped to persuade England to accept Presbyterianism. In this they were disappointed. They were successful, however, in obtaining freedom to exercise Presbyterian Church government in Scotland.

The main production of the Assembly was the Westminster Confession of Faith (1647), which laid down the Church's beliefs in all matters of doctrine – or, at any rate, what this gathering of earnest and sincere divines thought the Church ought to believe. It resembles to a great extent the Scottish Confession of 1560; and despite its dark, Calvinistic interpretation of much of Christ's teaching, it remains 'the chief subordinate standard' of my Kirk today.

In the considerably changed climate of modern social life and opinion moves are being made to produce a revised edition of the Westminster Confession. I should like to think that any new Confession might be less diffuse and doom-laden, as simple and clear as Christ's words in the New Testament. It might conclude, perhaps, with the punch-line: 'Love thy neighbour.' When scholars, priestly or otherwise, get excited about rules and regulations and, with highbrow zeal, elaborate upon them – the Confession runs to no less than thirty-three chapters – the people for whose benefit they are supposed to be created become confused and frustrated. They fret and argue and even fight among themselves, thus defeating the object of the exercise.

A similar thought may have been in the mind of Bishop Lancelot Andrewes when, in 1622, he preached to a congregation in London which included James VI and I. 'The nearer to the Church,' he said, 'the farther from God.'

I am glad that one day soon the Westminster Confession will be re-written. Like Calvin and others who have taken it upon themselves to call the numbers in a kind of religious bingo, in its present form it promises hairshirt salvation for God's 'elect', whoever they may be, and nothing but misery and eternal damnation for all those not 'elected'. (According to the Confession the Pope is definitely among the latter.) It speaks readily of giving love to God and dire punishments in store for people who neglect to do so. It speak less readily of giving love to man and the happiness and peace which this can bring.

As Cromwell assumed command of the country Scottish Presbyterianism appeared to have secured a lasting victory. The Solemn League and Covenant had been signed everywhere and many must have hoped that love and peace would settle at last upon a sorely harassed Scotland. As usual, they hoped in vain.

It now became a case of the stern, Calvinistic Covenanters, who wanted nothing at all to do with Episcopalian kings and prelates, versus the less bigoted Resolutioners, who were anxious to restore the monarchy and wanted to move the Kirk forward on more moderate lines. A subsidiary strand in the tangled skein was the still powerful presence, particularly in the Highlands and Islands, of several Roman Catholic clans.

When Charles I was put to death the Resolutioners seized an opportunity. They persuaded his son and heir to sign the Covenant and, at Scone in 1650, crowned him Charles II of Scotland. Oliver Cromwell, in complete command of England, was not amused. He immediately sent an army north. It defeated the Scots at Dunbar (1650) and finished off the short, sharp campaign by routing Charles II and his supporters at Worcester in 1651.

From then on Cromwell seemed to regard Scotland as a conquered country, to be moulded according to his will into the structure of the new commonwealth. In 1653, suspecting that it might become a political hindrance to his dictatorship, he disbanded the General Assembly.

All this caused resentment and anger among the proud, always nationalistic Scots. People who had admired and given him encouragement as a champion of Protestantism and

Presbyterianism turned against him. One of them was the Marquis of Montrose. He had signed the Covenant and fought for the Covenanters. Now, repelled by their grim, Old Testament attitudes, he turned his coat and fought for the rebellious but less inhibited and more colourful royalists.

Montrose was a true Scot, romantically inclined to impulsive action in pursuit of an ideal. Such action led him to a gallows erected in the High Street of Edinburgh where, on 21 May 1650, he was hanged as a rebel.

Like many another professional soldier, Field Marshal Viscount Wavell being one example, Montrose had poetry in his heart. Sixty-one years after his death some verses were published, said to have been written by him, though students of literature are now dubious about this claim. Whatever the truth, the poem entitled *My Dear and Only Love* (which was Scotland) reveals not only Montrose's character and aspirations but also his deeply felt but somewhat wry affection for his native country.

Here, as evidence, are three of its many stanzas.

> My dear and only love, I pray
>   This noble world of thee,
> As govern'd by no other sway
>   But purest Monarchy.
>
> He either fears his fate too much,
>   Or his deserts are small,
> That puts it not unto the touch,
>   To win or lose it all.
>
> But if thou wilt be constant then,
>   And faithful of thy word,
> I'll make thee glorious by my pen
>   And famous by my sword.

I wonder how many Scots, voting for or against a Scottish Assembly in 1979, remembered the words of that second stanza.

There is another poem by the third-century Gaelic hero Ossian (or by its eighteenth-century 'translator', James MacPherson), which contains a line, referring to the Celts: 'They went forth to battle but they always fell.' I think that, read together, the Lowland verses of Montrose and the Highland verses of Ossian provide valuable clues to the complex Scottish character. Present-day enthusiasts for Scotland in the world of sport – particularly in football – will understand what I mean.

Montrose's great rival among the nobles of Scotland was *Gillesbeag Gruamach* (Archibald of the Twisted Mouth). With his Campbell clansmen he gave unstinted support to the Covenanting army and was zealous in beating down the Roman Catholic clans, among which were the Campbells' traditional political enemies, the MacDonalds. But he too, like Montrose, paid the ultimate penalty for his zeal. When on Cromwell's death in 1658 the fabric of dictatorship fell speedily down, and the monarchy was restored in 1660, Argyll was arrested for 'compliance with the usurpation' and beheaded in Edinburgh.

During this long recital of Scottish history, encompassing four centuries, when many of the rulers and priestly scholars, ostensibly in the name of religion but in reality in a greedy scramble for personal and political power, were constantly at war with one another in a welter of hypocrisy and blood worse than in any video nasty, I have been trying to show the crudeness of the capers which attended the development of my Kirk. How, in the midst of it all, did Christianity survive?

It survived in the hearts and minds and actions of devoted men and women: some, from St Ninian onwards, whose names can never be forgotten, others unsung by 'religious' and secular historians. They needed no structured Church to teach them the truth, only the words of Christ in the New Testament. To their fellow beings they gave unselfish love when others gave only selfish hate.

Like sunlight lancing through stained-glass windows, Christianity continued to illumine the interior darkness of pulpit and pew.

14
The Baby and the Ring

At this point I am able, with some relief, to return to the grass-roots history of Southend at the Mull of Kintyre. Its religious condition during the centuries of strife remains obscure, though it is fairly certain that its ordinary folk – like ordinary folk in other parishes throughout Scotland – received little spiritual or social benefit from either Church or State.

Everywhere, except in the castles of feudal lords and in the palaces of prelates, the people suffered moral and physical poverty. Power play and the killings which resulted from it had to be paid for by somebody, and that somebody – as always – was the common man, often deliberately denied the education which might have shown him the extent to which his innocence and ignorance were being exploited. But in spite of every difficulty the human spirit is never completely stifled.

Reformation did reach Southend, despite the fact that, like the rest of Kintyre, most of its lands were occupied by the Roman Catholic MacDonald clan, proud descendants of the Lords of the Isles.

I have already told the story of the five *cailleachs* (or nuns) who, presumably, were found guilty of misdemeanours – connected, it may have been, with superstitious and even pagan practices – and expelled from *Caibel Carrine* to a lonely croft at the Mull.

Recently there has come to light more evidence that people in Southend, though far removed in a geographical sense from Knox's influence, were prepared to take angry action against what they perceived to be abuses in the Roman Church.

Near St Columba's footsteps at Keil, only a few metres away on the same green knoll, lies a flat slab of natural rock with a rectangular socket cut into it. On the north-east corner of the slab a tiny cross has been incised. The socket, I am told, once supported a 'prostration cross', beside which funeral processions, coming on foot to the burying ground, were accustomed to stop and rest near the end of their journey.

One October morning in 1978 my neighbour, Mary Taylor, was walking on the beach below the churchyard at Keil. The tide was unusually low and her eye was caught by a curiously shaped stone lying on an inshore reef. On examination she found it to be more than half the head of a wheel-cross, made of the local Old Red Sandstone.

Its interspaces were completely pierced. Carved in relief on the front was a worn representation of the crucified Christ. According to the Royal Commission on the Ancient and Historical Monuments of Scotland no precise parallels for this type of cross-head exist in Scotland, though it is obviously a late descendant of the Irish high cross. The Commission believes it to be more than 700 years old.

It is almost certain that this fragment was part of the cross which once stood in the rock socket on the knoll: a cross broken because people imagined it symbolized Rome and cast violently into the sea at the time of the Reformation.

That the censorious, anti-Roman spirit of John Knox reached Southend can be deduced from another small discovery, which I made myself.

For many years there hung in the porch of Southend Parish Church an artistically inscribed record of its ministers since the Reformation. The first name on the list was that of the Rev. Duncan Omey, who held the charge from 1611 to 1640. The second was that of the Rev. David Simson, 1672 to 1680.

I used to wonder why such a long time gap should exist between the two but put it down to the fighting which had occurred during this period between the MacDonalds and the Campbells. Disorder and chaos had reached a peak in 1647, when General David Leslie and his Covenanting army, assisted by the Marquis of Argyll and his clansmen, had laid siege to the MacDonalds in their castle on Dunaverty, across the bay from the church at Keil.

But then my wife's cousin, Andrew McKerral, showed me some notes he had taken from old records held by the Duke of Argyll at Inveraray Castle. To my surprise I found that

Southend actually did have a minister in the years immediately before the siege. His name was John Darroch, and he had served the parish from 1641 to 1646. Further investigation revealed that in 1646 he had summarily been deposed, for having had 'intercourse with the MacDonalds' and that the crime was considered so heinous that his name had been erased from all the Church records.

I felt sorrow and sympathy for John. Why shouldn't he have had 'intercourse' with his neighbours, Roman Catholic or not? I picture him as a friendly, guileless man, doing his best for love and peace in troubled times. That the Marquis of Argyll and other heritors (who, as contributers of tiends, paid stipends and had the power to manipulate all ministerial appointments) might object to his exchanging a word and a smile with other members of the small community, whatever their religious beliefs, probably never occurred to him.

There is no record of what happened to him after his deposition, though a vague local legend suggests that he left the district and became a farmworker on Jura.

Today the Church of Scotland has a care for all souls within the bounds of the parish, be they Christian or pagan, Roman Catholic, Protestant, Moslem or Hindu. And I am glad to say that a new list of the parish ministers of Southend now hangs in the porch of St Blaan's. John Darroch's name is writ large in second place.

In the complicated tapestry of Scotland's history, in which the secular and religious strands are never separate, the story of Dunaverty, culminating in the siege, is but one small line of stitches: a line, however, fitting closely into the main pattern. But in Southend's history the Rock has such a prominent place that the name crops up everywhere in the parish.

The community centre is Dunaverty Hall, which is also the home base of the Dunaverty Players Amateur Dramatic Club. There is the Dunaverty Golf Course occupied by the Dunaverty Golf Club. There are private houses called Dunaverty Lodge, Dunaverty House and Dunaverty Cottage. And the Rock itself, a lump of Old Red Sandstone about eighty metres high, overlooks Dunaverty Bay.

News of the Rock emerges from among the dawn clouds of knowledge. It was always a dun, a place of refuge against human and animal predators. During his short stay at the Mull of Kintyre St Columba may have walked across the sands of Dunaverty Bay to visit the family group whose home it was.

In the twelfth century the dun gave place to a castle: a castle held by Somerled's descendant, Angus Mor (Big Angus), son of Donald, from whom all MacDonalds derive their surname. Angus lost it for a time to Alexander III who, in turn, lost it to King Haco of Norway in 1263.

King Haco was a much more reasonable and statesmanlike 'viking' than many biased chroniclers have made out. In order to maintain good relations with the people of Kintyre and the numerous descendants of the Norsemen among them, he ultimately restored it to the MacDonalds.

Angus Mor's son, Angus Og (Young Angus) was a strong supporter of Robert the Bruce. After the disastrous Battle of Methven (1306) Bruce fled to Kintyre, where Angus Og gave him shelter. The future king was first hidden at Saddell Castle on the east coast of the peninsula, then in the more secure fortress of Dunaverty; and when even Dunaverty became unsafe he was taken secretly across the narrow sea to Rathlin, to another MacDonald castle inhabited, according to the legend, by at least one spider.

Angus Og was a king's man, and succeeding Lords of the Isles were king's men, too. But a time came when the kings began to realize that the MacDonald clan, wielding so strong an influence in the west, presented a dangerous threat to their overall authority in Scotland. When they tried to impose central government upon Argyll and the Isles the resentful MacDonalds, faced with the diminution of their power, withdrew their support from the monarchy.

Young James IV, impulsive as usual, decided to teach them a lesson. In 1494 he led to Kintyre an imposing army 'amply provided with artillery and gunners' and seized Dunaverty.

The MacDonalds struck back. At the time the representative of the clan in Kintyre was Sir John Cahanagh, a MacDonald by blood but so named from having been fostered in Antrim with a family of O'Cahans. He assembled an army of his own – in Kintyre, Islay and Antrim – and awaited his opportunity. The Rev. George Hill, the Irish historian, tells us what happened then: 'The King, not anticipating any opposition to his arrangements, was in the act of sailing away with his personal attendants from the Mull when Sir John stormed Dunaverty, and actually hung the governor from the wall, in sight of the King and his departing ships.'

A few years later the King had his revenge. Through the treachery of a kinsman, no doubt encouraged by a considerable bribe, Sir John and two of his sons were captured at Finlagan Castle in Islay and taken as prisoners to Edinburgh. There they were found guilty of high treason and 'executed on the Borrowmuir, their bodies being buried in the church of St Anthony'.

For the Lords of the Isles the tide of success began to ebb. Continually harassed by government troops, growing numbers of the clan crossed from Kintyre to Antrim, hoping to find there a more peaceable existence.

But peace and a lust for power are never compatible. When Mary became Queen of Scots the MacDonalds gave strong support to her cause. They wanted nothing to do with Protestantism. Besides, they saw an opportunity for their own advancement if Mary succeeded in establishing Roman Catholic rule in Scotland.

Now it was the turn of Elizabeth of England to teach them a lesson. She instructed her Irish Deputy, the Earl of Sussex, to deal severely with them, and deal severely with them he did. On 19 September 1558 he crossed with his army to Kintyre and burned 'twenty miles of its length', as well as the MacDonalds' 'chief house' at Saddell and their 'strong castell callit Dunalvere' (Dunaverty).

The situation was cruel and chaotic. Today it is mirrored in many other places.

By the beginning of the seventeenth century, despite the depredations carried out by the Earl of Sussex in the name of the law, the MacDonalds had repaired their castle on Dunaverty and were again a force to be reckoned with in Kintyre. But when Cromwell became the authority they found themselves in trouble once again, as royalists and rebels.

Their enemies, the Campbells, had taken up arms for Cromwell and the Presbyterian cause; and when General David Leslie was ordered to subdue the rebel MacDonalds in the west, the Marquis of Argyll eagerly accepted an invitation to

accompany him and to add a large quota of Campbell clansmen – 3000 according to one account – to an already considerable army. They marched through Dumbarton to Argyll and
down upon Kintyre.

Sir Alexander MacDonald made an effort to stop them at a
place called Rhunahaorine, a few miles south of Tarbert; but
his cavalry floundered to disaster in a peat-bog, and he and
most of his army were forced to retreat 'in small shippes' to
Islay.

A force of 300 men, however, 'consisting mainly of Mac-
Dougalls and soldiers from Antrim', was left behind to defend
Dunaverty. They were under the command of Archibald Og
MacDonald of Sanda, a direct descendant of Sir John Caha-
nagh, 'traitorously put to death by James IV'.

For six weeks Leslie and Argyll laid siege to the castle; but in
a hot, rainless June the water in the only well ran dry, as
occasionally it still runs dry in summer; and in the end it was
thirst that defeated the garrison. Archibald Og and his men
surrendered to 'the mercy of the kingdom', and the mercy of
the kingdom, as so often happened in that savage time, was
revealed as death.

'Every mother's son', wrote Sir James Turner, Leslie's ad-
jutant, 'was put to the sword, except one young man, Mac-
Coull [MacDougall], whose life I begged, to be sent to France,
with one hundred country fellows, whom we had smoked out
of a cave, as they do foxes.'

An account of the massacre given in the *Memoirs of Montrose* (Vol. II) brings a chill to the heart, resembling as it does
the more modern news from Northern Ireland. 'Having surrendered their arms the Marquis of Argyll and a bloody
preacher, Mr John Nevoy, prevailed with him [Leslie] to break
his word; and so the army was let loose among them, and
killed them all without mercy; whereat David Leslie seemed to
have some inward check: for, while the Marquis and he, Mr
Nevoy, were walking over their ankles in blood, he turned
about and said, "Now, Mass John, have you not, for once,
gotten your fill of blood?" This was reported by many who
heard it.'

John Nevoy was the minister of Loudon parish in Ayrshire,
a zealous Covenanter who had been appointed chaplain to

Leslie's army. He seems to have had little in common, as far as Christian feeling is concerned, with John Darroch, the recently deposed minister of Southend. John Darroch may have been saddened on leaving his people. But had he been allowed to stay and been forced to witness the carnage at Dunaverty his heart would most certainly have been broken.

The massacre is still spoken of in Southend as if it had happened yesterday. And more tales are told about it than appear in the historical records. They reveal to some extent the prevailing condition of ordinary folk whose moral and physical well being appeared to be of little interest to the rulers and the priestly scholars fighting violently amongst themselves for supremacy.

One such tale concerns the wife of a MacDonald soldier to whom the Campbells offered amnesty if, with her baby on her back, she could climb the sheer cliff on the east side of the Rock. She climbed it. But as her clutching hands appeared on the summit a young Campbell officer, laughing, slashed them off with his sword and she and her baby fell to their deaths. The cliff has a Gaelic name: The Cliff of the Falling Woman.

Next morning, with the castle burning, Leslie's army began to march away. As the Campbells, in the rear, were passing through the village of Southend (then called Muneroy), the young officer's horse reared and bolted. He was thrown from the saddle, but his foot caught in a stirrup and he was dragged, screaming for help, along the rough road beyond the village. His own men and the villagers who watched – all of them aware of his action on the previous day – gave no sign that they saw or heard. The horse ran free, swerving from side to side, dashing its rider to death against the boulders by the roadside.

Another tale is of the plague brought to Southend by Leslie's army. The nature of the plague is a matter of controversy between medical experts, though the majority opinion suggests typhus. It is said that hundreds of local people died of it . and that at one time, in the autumn of 1647, 'only two chimneys were left smoking' in the parish.

But yet another tale about Dunaverty offers happy evidence that beneath the smoke of death and destruction the light of Christianity continued to shine.

The wife of Archibald Og MacDonald, the commander of

the castle garrison, had died in the early part of 1647, leaving him with a baby son, James Ranald. James Ranald was with his father in the castle when the siege began, looked after by an eighteen-year-old Southend girl called Flora MacCambridge.

On the night before the massacre, putting no trust in 'the mercy of the kingdom', Flora made a plan to save the baby. Round him she wrapped a plaid of Campbell tartan which had belonged to a prisoner captured in the siege. Then, carrying him in her arms, she crept down from the Rock, and in the moonlight began to run across the beach, away from threatening death.

But soon, while stumbling over the wet, ribbed sand, she was stopped by a Campbell sentry. Her heart thumped in her throat.

'I am the wife of a Campbell soldier,' she said. 'See, my son wears the tartan.'

The sentry lifted a corner of the plaid. 'Strange!' he said. 'A Campbell mother whose baby has the MacDonald eyes! But go your way, girl. I have no quarrel with women or children.'

So Flora went to a cave under the cliff at Keil – adjacent to the little cave containing the 'Druid's' altar and less than 100 metres from St Columba's footsteps – and there, feeding him on sheep's tallow and ewe's milk, she hid and looked after James Ranald until the Campbells had gone.

James Ranald became a man. Eventually, by patient negotiation, he brought about a lasting peace between the MacDonalds and the Campbells in Kintyre. He lies buried in the churchyard at Keil.

One day, many years ago, a Mrs MacDonald from Zimbabwe (Southern Rhodesia) came to Southend to see the grave of her husband's ancestor. My father took her to Keil, showed her the flat, railed-in tombstone and then – as he so often did for the benefit of visitors – told her the story of Flora Mac-Cambridge. Finally he mentioned that James Ranald had married a daughter of the Stewarts of Bute.

The lady held out her left hand. 'I know,' she said. 'This is the ring he gave her.'

In a way I am personally involved in the story of Dunaverty. One of the 'hundred country fellows' smoked out of the cave at

Dunaverty and sent to France was called MacCaig. On his return from exile a few years later he met and married Flora MacCambridge. My wife Jean is their descendant.

15
Is the Kirk Christian?

Cromwell died. The dictatorship crumbled. In 1660 Charles II was given back his throne.

Having thus regained power in England, he calculated that Scottish support was no longer important to him. He broke his promise as a signatory of the National Covenant and, in his 'divine right' as a Stewart, did his utmost to ensure that Episcopacy was restored in Scotland.

Bishops were appointed. One of the foremost Resolutioners, James Sharp, was created Archbishop of St Andrews. Found guilty of treason, some of the most zealous Covenanters were executed. One of them was Johnston of Wariston. Another was the Earl of Argyll (*Gilleasbeag Gruamach*) who, at Scone on New Year's Day 1651, had crowned Charles as King of Scotland. A villain at Dunaverty, Argyll now took on the role of hero. On the night before his death he spoke quietly to a friend who had suggested suicide. 'I could die now like a Roman. But I choose rather to die tomorrow like a Christian.'

During this period the slowly emerging democratic nature of the Presbyterian Kirk was again under threat. In 1663 an Act was passed requiring attendance by all the people at services conducted by the Episcopalians. It was called, in some justice, the Bishop's Dragnet. Another Act – the Scots Mile Act – compelled Covenanting ministers to leave their parishes. In 1669 yet another Act was passed which may have caused John Knox to turn in his grave. This was the Assertory Act which claimed that the king was supreme in ecclesiastical as well as civil affairs. The Covenanters believed that 'the cloven hoof of Rome' was again being inserted in the door.

Episcopacy tended to flourish in the Highlands and in the north-east, mainly because the nobles and the big landowners in those regions considered it advisable, for their own material benefit, not to oppose the king. In the Lowlands generally, and in Ayrshire and the south-west in particular, most of the people rebelled against the new Acts. The 'outed' ministers took to the hills and moors, where they preached and celebrated the sacraments to large congregations.

It is recorded that on one occasion, at a remote and sheltered spot near the Whiteadder river, a conventicle was held at which 3000 people took communion. Five ministers took part, one of whom was John Welsh of Irongray, a great-grandson of John Knox. Episcopalian 'curates', some of them with characters and qualifications as dubious as those of the time-serving priests in medieval times, found their churches nearly empty.

Charles's government brought in the army to harry and subdue the recalcitrant Covenanters. As is usual in such a situation atrocities were committed on both sides.

In November 1666 soldiers arrested a Covenanter for refusing to attend an Episcopalian church in Galloway. His friends attacked them. One infuriated Presbyterian loaded a pistol with pieces of his tobacco pipe, fired it in a corporal's face and wounded him. The soldiers retreated. Encouraged, the crowd grew in numbers. They rode into Dumfries and captured Sir James Turner (chronicler of the massacre at Dunaverty) who commanded the troops in the district. Then they marched north to Ayr and Lanark and from there to Edinburgh, hoping to gather reinforcements on the way.

But support was meagre. Furthermore, the leaders of the crowd were mainly farmers and tradesmen who had no idea of how to conduct a battle, and their followers were almost all unarmed. At Rullion Green on the slopes of the Pentlands they were set upon by the dragoons of General Sir Thomas Dalziel and heavily defeated.

The authorities, however, were startled by this spontaneous uprising. They continued to persuade people to attend Episcopalian services; but for a time less physical force was used. This indulgent attitude made little impression on the strict mainline Covenanters. They still refused to take part in Episcopalian services and attended the hillside conventicles instead.

Gentler tactics having failed, the authorities reacted with

violence even more savage than before. Because the Covenanters always feared attack, they became accustomed to carrying arms at their conventicles. This gave the government an excuse to call such gatherings seditious rather than religious, and to describe their persecution of the Covenanters as punishment for breaking the law or, in certain cases, for treason. The twisted words of politicians are no new phenomenon.

Sir Walter Scott, though himself no great admirer of the Covenanters, was horrified by the actions of the persecuters. It was, he said, 'as if Satan himself had suggested means of oppression'. Farms were pillaged by troops sent to restore 'law and order'. Homes were invaded by dragoons and families thrown out to make room for billeting. Heavy fines were imposed, ruining many decent tradesmen. Hundreds of people whose only crime was a refusal to accept Episcopalianism were sent to prison.

Hideous tales concerning those times are still told in Scotland.

Sir Robert Grierson, laird of Lagg, is said to have held burning matches between the fingers of young girls to make them betray their Covenanting fathers and brothers. Dalziel, the victor of Rullion Green, threw women into pits containing frogs and snakes because they were loyal to their persecuted kinsfolk or supplied hunted refugees with food.

In 1679 a plot was hatched by twelve fanatical Presbyterians driven to the edge of madness by the continual persecution. The subject of their hate was James Sharp, who had once been their comrade in the Covenant but who now, having been appointed Archbishop of St Andrews (a blatant bribe?) had turned against them and was the instigator of much of the oppression. Led by John Balfour of Kinloch, the conspirators ambushed his coach on the Magus Moor, near St Andrews, dragged him from it and hacked him to death.

The story of John Brown is also told. He was a mild and harmless Ayrshireman who worked as a carter. He was also an unyielding Covenanter. One morning, on his way home, he was arrested by dragoons under the command of Graham of Claverhouse. He was led into the house, where his wife and children were waiting. Claverhouse gave him a few minutes to prepare himself for summary execution.

After saying his prayers John turned to his wife, Isobel, and asked her if she were willing to part with him. 'I am willing,' she whispered.

'That is all I could wish,' he said.

He gave her and the children his blessing and told Claverhouse he was ready. The dragoons held their fire. Perhaps John Brown's simple sincerity made them unwilling to murder him in cold blood. But Claverhouse – in the interests of military discipline, as he afterwards explained – drew his own pistol and shot John Brown through the head.

'What do you think of your husband now?' he asked Isobel.

'I aye thocht muckle o' him,' she said. 'But never sae muckle as I do this day.'

> To the Lords of Convention 'twas Claver's who spoke,
> 'Ere the king's crown shall fall there are crowns to be broke.'

For me, the glamour of Sir Walter Scott's song *Bonnie Dundee* has always turned tawdry when I remember the story of John Brown.

In 1681 Isabel Alison and Marion Harvey were condemned to death in Edinburgh for attending 'field preachings' and commenting adversely on the cruelty of the soldiers. On the scaffold they joined in singing Psalm 13, drowning the voice of the Episcopalian 'curate' who had been ordered to preach to them.

Marion Harvey was a domestic servant. She told the crowd that she was dying with a light heart. 'I am here today,' she said, 'for avowing Christ to be the head of His Church. I sought Him and I found Him. I found Him and will not let Him go!'

In 1685 Margaret MacLachlan and Margaret Wilson were tied to stakes in the Solway, near Wigton, and drowned as the tide-water rose, stubbornly refusing to deny their Covenanting beliefs. 'I am not afraid,' said Margaret Wilson. 'I am one of Christ's children.'

And during this period, what of the Covenant in my own parish, Southend?

After the massacre at Dunaverty, the Earl of Argyll seized power in Kintyre at the expense of the Clan Donald. He found it an easy conquest because many of the Roman Catholic

Highlanders in the district had been killed or had died of the plague or fled to Ireland. From Renfrewshire, Ayrshire and other parts of the south-west he brought to his deserted lands Covenanting farmers who would not only cultivate the ground profitably but also support him faithfully in his Protestant, Presbyterian activities. In the history of Kintyre this has been called the Lowland Plantation.

Families of Ralstons, Reids, Pickens, Caldwells and Browns (as well as many others) began to populate Southend alongside the established families of MacDonalds, MacKays, MacMurchys, MacShannons and McKerrals. The natives were suspicious of their new neighbours, who were inclined to regard themselves as superior in both a religious and a social sense, and for a time harsh divisions existed between them. Indeed, the Lowlanders refused to bury their dead in the same ground as the Highlanders – around the old church at Keil – and took over a piece of land, formerly a vegetable garden, which lay immediately to the west of the existing cemetery.

One of the first Lowlanders to be buried in the new ground was William Ralston who, in his youth, had been involved as a fighting man with the Covenanters in Renfrewshire. Among the ranks of gravestones in the present 'old' cemetery, all facing the east and rising sun according to pagan custom, his is the only one which faces north. This is because, on his deathbed, the tough old Covenanter gave an order to his family: 'Bury me wi' ma back tae Rome!'

The Highland and Lowland burying-grounds at Keil used to be separated by an open stream running shorewards from St Columba's Well. But time passed. Lowland lass married Highland chiel and Highland maid married Lowland lad. Religious bigotry was stifled by family love. Slowly but surely divisions became blurred.

Descendants of Lowlanders and Highlanders now live at peace together, the blood of Ralstons and Reids, MacDonalds and MacKays all happily intermingled. And the stream in the cemetery has been covered over and hidden in a culvert.

History depends so much on dates and battles and on the names and reputations of leaders both secular and religious that the roots of my Kirk, from the outline I have tried to give, may appear to have been planted in noxious and extremely unpromising soil. But I find it important to remember that though the Church at various times has capered violently under the influence of power and party politics, individual men and women continued to heed the words of Christ in the New Testament, thus keeping the Church always mindful of its pact with Christianity.

It seems to me that too many people nowadays equate Christianity with the Church. This is an error. The Church is a man-made edifice. Christianity is entirely of the spirit.

To keep Christianity alive amid the chaos there must have been many individuals who by their example kept the light of Christianity burning and encouraged the efforts of leaders in the Church to keep it on a straight road. If we could see through the bloody mist of time we should be able to identify and give credit to such people: unknown and unrecorded Ninians, Columbas, Elphinstones, Luthers, Hamiltons and Knoxes.

Sometimes we catch a glimpse of them: the literate scribe who composed the Arbroath Declaration, the poet Dunbar, the nursemaid Flora MacCambridge, the domestic servant Marion Harvey. And the aristocrat's daughter, Lady Grizel Baillie.

Grizel Hume was born on Christmas Day, 1665, eldest of eighteen children born to Sir Patrick and Lady Hume of Polwarth. When only twelve years old she was employed as a kind of juvenile undercover agent, carrying secret messages between her father and Robert Baillie of Jerviswood, who, at the time, as a militant Covenanter, was in prison in Edinburgh. While carrying out one of these dangerous missions she met George Baillie, Robert's son, and a love story began.

When Robert Baillie was executed, his friend, Sir Patrick Hume, was also denounced as a rebel. The Hume estates were forfeited and he went into hiding, his refuge being a vault in the parish kirk at Polwarth, a mile or two away from Redbraes Castle where the family lived. Every night Grizel faced the dark terrors of the churchyard to bring her father food, encouragement and news of happenings at home.

One evening troopers were in the castle, searching for its elusive owner. With a view to taking it out later to give to her father, Grizel had hidden the greater part of her dinner in her lap. Suddenly one of her younger brothers began to draw the troopers' attention to what he imagined was his big sister's greed.

'Will you look at Grizel? While we've been supping our broth she's eaten a whole sheep's head!'

Happily the troopers were too busy to pay much attention to a small boy.

In the end, Sir Patrick and his family were able to escape to Holland. As Lady Hume was an invalid, Grizel made all the arrangements for the journey.

A week or so later she returned to Scotland to collect her little sister Gillian, who was ill and had been left behind. When the two girls landed at Brielle on the Dutch coast nobody was there to meet them. They had to walk to Rotterdam, and for most of the way Grizel carried Gillian on her back.

In Utrecht, where they finally settled, Grizel managed the household while her father earned a small income by practising as a doctor.

One day another Covenanting fugitive from Scotland arrived on their doorstep. (Since the time of Erasmus Holland has always been a Protestant haven.) He was George Baillie, who had never forgotten 'the wee Hume lassie' he had met in Edinburgh. He lived with the family for three and a half years, boisterous, gallant, head over heels in love with Grizel. He and Patrick, the youngest son of the house, enlisted together as guardsmen under the Prince of Orange.

Those years, according to Grizel, were the happiest of her life. Though the household was in poverty she sang at her work and even found time to write her own songs. Perhaps because her own love affair was happy and uncomplicated, these were often about tragic lovers.

> When bonny young Johnny cam' ower the sea
> He vowed he saw naething sae lovely as me.
> He gi'ed me gowd rings and mony braw things –
> And werena my he'rt licht I wad dee.

But in this sad song the recurring last line does suggest something of Grizel's own patience, courage and good humour in face of misfortune.

And in her case, such patience, courage and good humour

were to be rewarded. When William of Orange acceded to the throne of Britain Sir Patrick Hume's estates were returned to him. So were those of George Baillie, and in 1692 he and Grizel were married.

They had three children and lived in solid style, pillars of Kirk and State. But long afterwards, when she was a widow, still helping and looking after her numerous relatives, Lady Grizel told her daughter that she would have been quite content to live with her husband 'on bread and water on the top of a mountain'.

She was buried beside him on Christmas Day, 1746.

16
'Dissidence of Dissent'

Charles II died in 1685. His brother, who had served as Lord High Admiral of England in the Dutch wars, came to the throne as James VII of Scotland and II of England.

Like Charles, James believed in the divine right of kings. Unlike Charles, who could be a Covenanter, an Episcopalian and even a friend of Rome whenever it suited his plans for power, James was unambiguously Roman Catholic. Under his influence the persecution of the Covenanters in Scotland became even more cruel.

With only one or two notable exceptions Scottish Episcopalian leaders approved James's persecuting measures; but their fawning support of the Crown's drive against popular liberty and the rights of the Kirk marked the beginning of the end of Episcopalian ascendancy in Scotland.

This second deliverance of the Scottish Kirk began in England. James's arbitrary acts against the constitution and the Church roused the indignation of the predominantly Protestant English people. Seven leading politicans approached William, Prince of Orange – whose wife was Mary, James's daughter – and appealed to him as a good soldier and committed Protestant to rescue them from what they imagined to be a cunning effort to return England to the dominance of France and Rome.

With a powerful army of 15,000 English and Dutch soldiers William landed at Torbay on 4 November 1688. The people hailed him as a saviour. Deserted by his troops and even by close relatives, James fled. For a time some of his adherents held out in Scotland, among them John Graham of Claverhouse, Viscount Dundee. But at the Pass of Killiecrankie, on 27 July 1689, his men were routed by General Mackay and resistance to King William virtually came to an end.

'Bonnie Dundee' himself was killed at Killiecrankie, struck in the body by a musket-ball. Today he would be called a mercenary, willing to fight for anybody who paid him well enough. Religious considerations did not worry him. By a strange irony, one of his first 'contracts' was in Holland as a cornet in Prince William's horse-guards. It is said that during a battle fought at Seneff in 1647 he saved the prince's life.

On 13 February 1689 William and Mary were proclaimed King and Queen of England. In April of the same year the Convention of Estates offered them the throne of Scotland, provided Episcopacy were abolished as ' a great and insufferable grievance and trouble to the nation, and contrary to the inclinations of the generality of the people, ever since the Reformation (they having reformed from Popery to Presbyters)'.

Having been brought up in Holland in a Church that was similar to that of Scotland under Presbyterianism, William was sympathetic to this idea. In any case, his chief adviser in Scottish religious affairs was William Carstares (1649–1715), a minister's son and staunch Presbyterian who had suffered persecution and even physical torture by the Episcopalians. The new sovereign agreed to 'settle by law that Church government in this kingdom [Scotland] which is most agreeable to the people'.

Accordingly Episcopacy was set aside and the Presbyterian system, first inaugurated in 1592, was revived. 'Outed' ministers were restored to parishes. The theory of the divine right of kings was spiked and buried, hopefully once and for all. When Union between Scotland and England took place in 1707 the Kirk gave support to it reluctantly and only on condition that the National Kirk should remain Presbyterian and retain all its religious liberties.

To this day, at the coronation, one of the first acts of any British sovereign is to sign a promise to protect and maintain the Church of Scotland.

A new word now entered the vocabulary of religion: toleration. It was inserted by King William. In his letter to the Kirk's General Assembly of 1690 he offered some salutary advice: 'We could never be of the mind that violence was suited to the advancing of true religion . . . Moderation is what religion enjoins, neighbouring Churches expect from you, and we recommend to you.'

A new philosophy was also beginning to have an effect upon the leaders of the various Churches. This was most clearly expressed, perhaps, by John Locke in 1689: 'No man is hurt because his neighbour is of a different religion from his own, and no civil society is hurt because its members are of different religions from one another.'

But after such a long history of bigotry and blame, of death and destruction, the Scots found it difficult to realize that the democratic liberty which had been their holy grail was now within their grasp. They were eager advocates of Christianity. In the aftermath of violence, however, as frail human beings, many of them still failed to offer one another Christian love.

This, rather than the nine of diamonds, has always been the curse of Scotland. (As it has been, of course, in most other countries.) Instead of speaking together, with one powerful voice, we have quarrelled and squabbled and whined among ourselves, often in pursuit of personal material gain, thus allowing inimical forces, both spiritual and physical, to exploit division and hold us in subjection. In simple words Christ told us how to achieve unity. We have paid lip service to his teaching; but in the nation as a whole, and even in my Kirk, the rulers and priestly scholars have clouded the vision with so much argument and 'interpretation' that it tends to appear and disappear like a phantom in the mists of the Cairngorms.

From the beginning of the eighteenth century the fighting, the tortures, the burnings and the executions ceased, except during the brief Stewart rebellions of 1715 and 1745. These, though nationalistic, had no great religious significance. But public arguments continued to take place in which the resulting harm was moral rather than physical.

Many of them raged within the Kirk itself. For example, the Resolutioners and the Protesters who had once aimed physical violence at one another were now replaced by Moderates and Evangelicals who fought with verbal weapons. The chief sources of such intellectual strife were Theology, which expounded 'the science of things divine', the problem of authority versus the individual conscience and, of course, the question of the relation between Church and State, which may be said to have included the vexing factors of patronage.

The Moderates were free-thinkers inclined to look down their Roman noses at the supernatural aspects of the Christian story. The Evangelicals were the successors of the Covenanters, strict Calvinists who believed in damnation and hell for 'unelected' sinners but who, nevertheless, were emphatic that the gospel message should be offered freely to all. The Moderates looked upon the Evangelicals as bleak and narrow. The Evangelicals looked upon the Moderates as careless in their beliefs and even, in some cases, heretical.

The trouble about eighteenth- and nineteenth-century Evangelical thought was that it encouraged the idea that some people were 'chosen' by God. It appears that to be thus 'chosen' (or 'elected') the person concerned had simply to declare his or her 'state of grace' in public. Private sins ought then to be forgiven and overlooked. Through such an idea there percolated echoes of the Roman Catholic theory of confession, by which a priest or a Pope, rather than God, purges and forgives a person's sin. Inevitably it contained the bitter seeds of hypocrisy.

Robert Burns was an honest man. Like everybody else he was a sinner; but he had neither the gall nor the arrogance to try to conceal his sins under a blanket of declared 'grace'. He was condemned by the 'unco guid' and on one occasion, as a member of the Church, was made to occupy 'the stool of repentance' at a Sunday-morning service.

Naturally, he had no great regard for some of his accusers, who, like himself, were often 'fash'd wi' fleshly lust'. He wrote about them in a satirical poem entitled 'Holy Willie's Prayer':

> Lord, bless Thy chosen in this place,
> For here Thou hast a chosen race!
> But God confound their stubborn face,
> And blast their name,
> Wha bring Thy elders to disgrace,
> An' open shame.

In my Kirk today arguments between 'Moderates' and 'Evangelicals' are far from over, and many a 'holy Willie' can still be identified. I believe, however, that on both sides

Christ's plea for love and understanding among saints and sinners is having an ever-increasing effect. The tangled under-growth is withering and the bright bush is emerging fresh and beautiful. Happiness and laughter, the products of shared love, are taking the place of doom and gloom and intellectual turmoil.

Would Calvin have choked upon his Sunday supper if he had lived to hear some of the stories that are now told in Scottish churches? One of them concerns a Highland minister who was preaching violently about hell — 'And there shall be weeping and wailing and g-nashing of teeth' — when suddenly, in a pew immediately in front of the pulpit, he caught sight of an old gentleman with no teeth at all, who was smiling a wide and naked smile. The minister scarcely paused. 'As for you, my friend,' he said, '*teeth will be provided!*'

This may seem a humorously exaggerated story in our modern, more sophisticated and 'liberal' society; but in Scot-land in the eighteenth century — and even less than a hundred years ago — it could have happened.

There is a family story concerning my great-grandfather in North Uist. Old Angus was an elder in the Church of Scotland but had the reputation of being fairly liberal in both religion and politics. Trudging towards church one Sunday morning, he encountered on the road a neighbour of his, an extreme Evangelical, who was heading for a church in a different direction. 'A fine day, Donald!' he greeted him. Donald shook his head in grim disapproval. 'This is not a day, Angus, to be speaking of days!'

When deeply felt religious arguments occur the antagonists often move farther and farther apart until extreme and some-times ridiculous positions are occupied by both sides. The same thing happens in politics. In our own time democratic arguments concerning capitalism and socialism have tended to degenerate into arguments concerning fascism and commun-ism. All this is understandable, in human terms, when vio-lence, either physical or moral, has been used to support the arguments. Memories of persecution die hard, and the quiet voice advising us to love our neighbour is diminished by shouts of 'No surrender!'

The Scottish Presbyterians had endured centuries of

suffering to achieve their goal of a democratic form of church government, with God rather than any temporary ruler as its Head. Is it any wonder that they came to believe that true Christianity could only be achieved by threatening suspected opponents with dire and awful divine punishments?

But since the message of love was first brought to Scotland there have been quiet people who, in the midst of strife, kept the Christian spirit of the Church alive. One of them had a connection with Southend. He was Professor John Simson, the close relative of a Southend minister.

Simson taught theology at Glasgow University. He dealt in reason rather than in blind faith. Christ's teaching, he said, showed mankind the best possible way of life. What he failed to emphasize was Christ's divinity, and because of this, in 1714, he was advised by the General Assembly to be more careful about what he said.

But, like the Bishop of Durham in our own time, he continued to preach the importance of practical Christianity in relation to society and was outspoken about the lack of love and compassion shown by the stern Calvinists. Nor could he find love or logic in the doctrine favoured by some Evangelicals: a doctrine which held that 'the chosen of God' – the Bible-quoters, the pillars of public 'holiness', the loud 'praise the Lord' churchgoers – could sin to their heart's content in private and yet call themselves Christian.

In 1729, under pressure from the Evangelicals, Simson was accused of heresy by the General Assembly and, after a lengthy inquiry, suspended from teaching. A hundred years earlier he might have been executed or burned at the stake. So might the Bishop of Durham, even now, did he not live in an age when people have been educated to think for themselves and to favour democracy in both Church and State.

In the early eighteenth century the unified Parliament still struggled to retain authority over the Scottish Church and its spiritual freedom. In 1712 it passed the Patronage Act, which was unwanted by the Church and a palpable breach of the Treaty of Union. (Breaches of the Treaty, most of them to the disadvantage of Scotland, have occurred frequently down the years. They still do. But that is another story.)

The Patronage Act set aside the democratic principle whereby 'the Christian people or society of believers who join in full communion together are the persons who, according to the New Testament, have a right to elect their minister'. In effect, it restored the old authoritarian practice by which clergymen were chosen by the landowners, who had a duty to build churches and pay the ministers.

To begin with, the Act did not cause too much trouble. Some of the 'landowners' were now Crown officials and burgh councillors, who, sensibly, made it a habit to consult local opinion when choosing a minister. But there remained powerful rulers – sometimes in league with priestly scholars – who took full advantage of their position and made sure that the appointment of ministers remained their prerogative. In my own parish, Southend, six out of the eight ministers appointed during the period 1696 to 1880 were Campbells. The choice, in general, was that of a Duke of Argyll, chief of the Clan Campbell.

Gradually it began to dawn on more and more members of the Kirk that the religious democracy for which their forefathers had fought so stoutly was, in a Church thirled to the State, in danger of erosion. Their ideas were stimulated by news of the French Revolution and by the growing surge of anti-authoritarian thought in England which reached its height with the Reform Act of 1832. Robert Burns also had influence. His poems and songs were a 'programme of social and political reform and progress, or at any rate, aspiration'. 'A man's a man for a' that,' he declared bluntly.

People nursed an uneasy feeling that some ministers, though often worthy and even saintly men, were being appointed not always to ensure the spiritual well being of the local congregation but often to ensure the temporal well being of the 'landlord' and his Establishment friends.

Arguments along such lines were like the ticks of a clock connected to numerous time-bombs. During the next century the Kirk was rocked by a series of explosions which dented its structure and left debris lying about in pathetic confusion. Love and peace, the desire of ordinary people through the ages – the shining gifts of Christ – were obscured and overladen in clouds of the resultant dust.

As each explosion occurred the main edifice of the Kirk – the

Established Presbyterian Church of Scotland – remained stand-
·ing, though always vulnerable to further fragmentation because of the Patronage Act.

To list in detail and to identify specific local reasons for all
the secessions and sub-secessions which took place between
1690 and the present day would require several volumes and
an author more skilled in Church history than I am. But to
demonstrate the complexity and confusion of the situation I
will try to summarize them.

Fasten all safety-belts.

From the outset, in 1690, some people in the Kirk refused to
accept the Revolution Settlement. They were the Camero-
nians, named after Richard Cameron, an extreme Evangelical
who, in Sanquhar (Dumfriesshire) in 1680, had declared a
private war against Charles II as a tyrant and an enemy of the
Covenants. His little 'army' was attacked on Ayres Moss by a
company of dragoons and Cameron was killed.

But he had established a strong following which, in 1773,
became the Reformed Presbyterians, though the name Cam-
eronians persisted. Until 1876, when a large majority joined
the Free Church, the Reformed Presbyterians had a dour and
rock-like solidity, despite the paucity of their numbers. A tiny
fragment of their Church still exists.

The Established Church did not for long remain so rock-
like. In 1733 there occurred a major secession which resulted
in a Church calling itself at first the Associate Synod (or
Burghers) and, later, the United Secession. This, in turn, threw
off two fragments: the Anti-Burghers in 1747 (otherwise
known as the General Associate Synod) and the Auld Lichts
(Old Lights or Original Associate Synod) in 1799.

But – wait for it and concentrate – in 1800 the General
Associate Synod fragment threw off a sub-fragment calling
itself the Original Old Lights (a primmer mode of speech was
now creeping in). This soon became more than a sub-fragment
and established itself as the Church of the Original Secession in
1842.

A curious and isolated event occurred in 1830, when a
majority of the Original Associate Synod (the Old Burghers as
they were called by their opponents, often with the 'r' left out)
united in holy love with the Established Church. At the same

time the minority united with the General Associate Synod (anti-Burghers) which now came to be known as the United Original Secession.

Meanwhile, the Established Church had experienced another secession in 1761, when a Relief Synod was formed. The reason for the breakaway, as always, was the threat to liberty imposed by the Patronage Act.

The daft caperings which went on at this time between Church and State are well illustrated by what happened in Southend.

In 1794 the Rev. Donald Campbell was presented to the parish by the Duke of Argyll. From the beginning Donald was at loggerheads with certain members of his session and congregation. They complained that his preaching was 'unedifying', that as a parish minister he was 'frivolous' and, worst of all, that he had been installed in Southend by the duke against their wishes.

Donald took a courageous stand against such accusations. He deposed and excommunicated three of the elders in his session, summoned one of them to appear on charges of defamation of character and demanded a visitation of the Presbytery of Kintyre. No doubt in an effort to obtain peace – if not love – the Presbytery approved and confirmed the minister's course of action.

All this was reported to the duke who, through his law agent, surprisingly took the side of the rebels. He withdrew his support from his namesake and summarily transferred him from Southend to the parish of Kilninver, near Oban. The rebels, according to the law agent, had been 'much misrepresented' and were among 'the most intelligent and respected persons in the parish'. Significantly, most of them were tenants of the duke's farms, paying high rents.

The rebels in Southend now intimated that they wanted to build a church and a manse in the village. To their delight the duke offered them land for the purpose, along with a glebe of thirteen acres. What they did not realize was that at the time the duke was planning an extension of the village, and the building of a church and manse fitted well into his scheme. The new village did not, in the end, materialize; but the new church and manse did. Thus one of the first rural Relief congregations in Scotland was founded.

(I am happy to report that in 1826 Edinburgh University made the Rev. Donald Campbell a Doctor of Divinity. He may not have been all that 'frivolous'.)

In 1843 the greatest explosion of all rocked the Church of Scotland. The cause was again the clash of Moderates and Evangelicals, the Moderates holding that the State (or 'land-owners') should have some say in the running of the Church, the Evangelicals arguing that State control was endangering not only the 'purity' of the Church (from a Biblical point of view) but also the spiritual independence of individual members.

For some time the Moderates had ruled the General Assembly, though their belief in the principle of State control must have been shaken by the number of secessions which had taken place because of it. Now, however, the Evangelicals became even more vociferous, claiming that State laws such as those contained in the Patronage Act ought to be set aside in favour of laws initiated by the Church.

Their frustration grew when the law courts ruled against the Veto Act, which, against opposition, they had forced the General Assembly to pass in 1835. The Act had stated : 'It is a fundamental law of the Church that no pastor shall be intruded in any congregation contrary to the will of the people.'

At about the same time the Oxford Movement was founded in England. Its aim was also to do away with State interference in religious affairs.

In the Highlands of Scotland many people had become disillusioned with a Church thirled to civil government. In some measure this was because of the Clearances, when absentee landlords, many of them living in England, authorized their local representatives to get rid of 'unprofitable' crofters and fill their estates with 'profitable' sheep. The Napoleonic wars had caused a steep rise in the price of wool.

With only a few honourable exceptions, ministers supported the 'landowners', condoning the evictions as being an expression of God's will and praying with holy unction for the crofters' moral safety and material success in far countries.

The ministers owed their comfortable livings to the State and the Establishment. Christian love and care did not seem to enter into their calculations.

Party politics was another factor in the Kirk situations, as it always had been and still is. Successive prime ministers, Lord Melbourne and Sir Robert Peel, were, predictably, against the Church gaining too much power at the expense of the State.

One of the Scots ministers prominent in the long struggle for freedom in the Kirk was the Rev. Thomas Chalmers, a native of Fife and a graduate of St Andrews University. He had a broad Scots accent and a cultured, questioning mind. In his lifetime he produced thirty-four books, most of them on the subject of theology but others with unexpected, down-to-earth titles, such as *Enquiry into Natural Resources* and *Commercial Discourses*. Like St Columba he believed that religion and everyday, workaday life are inextricably mixed and that a spiritual profit should always be sought in preference to a material one.

Chalmers's eloquence as a preacher was, in the words of J.G. Lockhart, 'capable of producing an effect ... strong and irresistible'. He began his ministry in the little country parish of Kilmany, then served for a time as minister of the Tron Church in Glasgow. Like Tom Allan, another great and good minister of the Tron in modern times, Thomas Chalmers inspired not only deep affection in friends and colleagues but also admiration for his organizational abilities, even among those like Melbourne and Peel who disliked and opposed him.

In 1823 he accepted the Chair of Moral Philosophy at St Andrews University. Four years later he became Professor of Theology at Edinburgh.

But his greatest achievement had a memorable date, 1843, and a memorable name, the Disruption.

That year, thwarted by Parliament and hindered by Moderates in his efforts to nullify the Patronage Act, he stood up in the General Assembly in Edinburgh and led out his Evangelist supporters. From St Andrew's Church in George Street they marched in procession to the Tanfield Hall in Canonmills, where, amidst fiery enthusiasm, the Free Church of Scotland was founded.

About a third of the Kirk membership seceded with him. So
did 474 ministers out of a total of 1203. Those ministers
surrendered their parishes, their manses and their stipends,
all in the cause of upholding the spirit of liberty and, what
was even more important to them, 'the Crown rights of the
Redeemer'.

Chalmers was the first Moderator of the Free Church
Assembly; and not long before he died in 1847 he became
Principal of the Free Church College. Thanks to his skill as an
orator and organizer – and thanks to a generous membership –
the 'striking' ministers were soon preaching in new churches
and living comfortably in new manses.

For many years after the Disruption currents of bitterness
swirled between the Church of Scotland, the Auld Kirk as it
was known, and the Free Kirk, later nicknamed the Wee Frees.
No doubt harbouring twinges of guilt that they appeared to
concede to the State an authority equal to God's, Auld Kirkers
argued that a Church with completely independent jurisdiction might lead to a theocracy as dangerous as state autocracy:
a theocracy which would be too much concerned with the
punishment of sinners and not enough with their redemption.
The Free Kirkers argued that the Auld Kirkers were time-
serving and 'lightsome' in their spiritual beliefs.

As a result of such feuding, ministers and some members on
both sides vied with one another to exhibit their 'holiness'.
Biblical texts were bandied about, many from the Old Testament, some – often out of context – from the New. Unction
was rife. Human love cowered under torrents of 'holy'
words.

I remember a stout divine from the far north who came
to assist my father at a Communion service in Southend.
He preached hell-fire for those who drank to excess and
who 'fornicated even in their imagination' and then had
three helpings of rich plum-pudding at lunch, leaving my
mother with none. Later, with evident sorrow for her
soul, he called her a 'frivolous and godless creature'
because she gathered some flowers from the garden on a
Sabbath afternoon.

My brothers and I, not yet in our teens, had at the time the
mistaken but popularly held idea that Christianity and the

Church were synonymous. We loved our mother; and on that Sunday we all took a poor view of Christianity.

As the years passed, however, the spirit of self-sacrifice and loyalty to principle shown by the seceders had its influence on the Auld Kirk. And the spirit of tolerance and care for the social well being of the people shown by the Auld Kirk had its influence on the Wee Frees. More and more people had access to education. More and more people learned to read the New Testament for themselves and became more concerned with the Christian message of 'love one another' than with legalistic and 'holy' rivalry.

In 1852 a majority of the Original Seceders joined the Free Church. In 1876 a majority of the Reformed Presbyterians joined the Free Church. But, as happened in Southend, the United Secession Church, now calling itself the United Presbyterian Church, soldiered on until 1900, when it was joined by a majority of the Free Church and became the United Free Church.

The idea of Union became sweet. The will for union became strong. It was conveyed from congregations, through Presbyteries and Synods to the General Assemblies.

In 1929, as Christianity and common sense broke through to repair man-made divisions, the Church of Scotland and the United Free Church at last came together, casting aside, with relief, most of the lingering effects of the Patronage Act. Though a few splinters still remained, notably twelve Presbyteries of the Free Church, in general my Kirk was whole again. Its heart was not now in high and holy places but in small communities and congregations.

In Southend it was my father's privilege to be the first minister of a united parish. There was happiness, as at a family reunion. Some rulers and priestly scholars may have been somewhat miffed that their power and glory had been delivered into the hands of the people. But I am sure that the ghosts of our ancestors – Mesolithic and Neolithic men, Bronze Age and Iron Age men, Picts and Scots and Norsemen, Covenanters and Royalists, Seceders and Auld Kirkers – all looked on with approval.

There is one ghost in Southend who must have smiled, adjusted his somewhat crooked halo and then stepped on to the footsteps rock at Keil to shout with joy: the ghost of Columba, who spoke for Christ.

17
Who – or What – is God?

Did John R. Gray have the patience to read thus far (which I doubt), he would now confront me with brusque words: 'I didn't want your views on religious history, especially as I don't necessarily agree with all of them. I wanted you to tell me what your convictions are about Man and God. In short, what you believe, as a professing Christian.'

To which, with as much confidence as I could muster, I might reply: 'My beliefs about Man and God have taken shape through the study of religious history, the record of Man's relations with God throughout the centuries.'

Bravely ignoring John's obvious doubts concerning my scholarship, I would then go on to explain that I had felt it necessary to set down all the complicated evidence which has led me towards certain conclusions.

The Church has little to do with stone and lime. It consists of people. I believe that the history of my Kirk, being also the history of the people of Scotland, may be looked upon as a parable: a parable indicating the wrong roads and the right roads in our long, laborious search for God.

But who – or what – is God?

I believe that inside every human being there exists the desire to worship a caring God. 'I came from nothing,' wrote Alice Meynell, 'but from where come the undying thoughts I bear?'

The Neolithic men and the Bronze Age men had their sun god. They built their altars facing east; and when the chiefs swore fealty to the tribe they stood on a carved stone and made their vows to him. The Bronze Age Melanesians had a god called Qat. The Babylonians had Baal. The Greeks and Romans worshipped Jupiter. The Jews prayed to Yahweh.

In the Christian era men have worshipped an 'Ancient of Days' on a cumulus cloud, a white-bearded old gentleman frowning down at our capers 'here below'. Francis Thomson imagined Him as a 'steep and trifid' being, a stern High King of Heaven sitting in judgement on us all when we die.

A drunk man staggers and mutters, 'God help us!' A Sloane Ranger exclaims, on television, 'My God!' A dramatic critic denigrates a stage play with the words, 'For God's Sake!' A little girl in an aircraft climbing higher and higher above the clouds clutches her mother's arm. 'Maybe we'll see God!' she whispers excitedly. To whom – or to what – do they refer?

Sometimes we are inclined to worship gods to whom we can relate in material terms. They may include sporting stars, pop stars, business tycoons, leaders of the armed forces, actors and writers. Even politicians. But all these are chancy gods, revered when things are going well, unloved when things go wrong. They fall far short of our instinctive conception of a God who cares for all of us rather than for a favoured few.

> The Lord, ye know, is God indeed.
> Without our aid he did us make.

The Psalmist poses a problem. He may have believed that God was a super manufacturer working with some kind of supercharged plasticine. But I think he was merely indicating his belief that Man was separate from God. Even so, I cannot bring myself to share his belief.

The Shorter Catechism was approved in 1648 by the General Assembly of the Church of Scotland. It was described as 'a Directory for catechising such as are of weaker Capacity'. Most of us who attended Sunday School in the early part of this century must have been considered by the priestly scholars to have been of 'weaker Capacity', because we all had to learn it by heart and repeat it, word for ponderous word, to our teachers on a Sabbath morning.

I do not need to check its definition of God: I remember it with stark clarity: 'God is a spirit, infinite, eternal and un-changeable, in his being, wisdom, power, holiness, justice, goodness and truth.' This helps me to understand; but I still cannot go along with the idea that God is separate from Man.

The theologians confuse me. What do the poets and the scientists have to say about God?

> There have been so many gods
> That now there are none.
> When the one God made a monopoly of it
> He wore us out,
> So now we are godless
> And unbelieving.

I suppose we must allow D.H. Lawrence a vision of despair. but, like all poets, he had other visions. He writes thus about peace.

> Sleeping on the hearth of the living world,
> Yawning at home before the fire of life,
> Feeling the presence of the living God
> Like a great reassurance,
> A deep calm in the heart,
> A presence
> As of the master sitting at the board
> In his own and greater being,
> In the house of life.

Is there a hint here of a definition, a poet's mystic understanding of what God may be?

'But God, if a God there be, is the substance of men, which is man.' This strikes a chord in my mind. It seems to me that Charles Algernon Swinburne (of all people) offers a bridge between a poet's vision and the analytical view of the scientist.

More than half way across the bridge I encounter Pierre Teilhard de Chardin, who was a scientist as well as a priest. 'By a perennial act of communion and sublimation, man aggregates to himself the total pantheism of the earth. And when he has gathered everything together and transferred everything, he will close in upon himself and his conquests, thereby rejoining, in a final gesture, the divine focus he had never left. That, as St Paul tells us, God shall be all in all . . . The reflective centres of the world are effectively no more than "one with God". This state is obtained not by identification (God becoming all) but by the differentiating and communicating action of love (all God in everyone).'

Teilhard de Chardin believed that we, mankind, contain in

ourselves the possibilities of earth's immense future and can realize more and more of those possibilities on condition that we increase our knowledge and our love.

Anaxagoras, the philosopher, lived in Greece 500 years before Christ was born. 'In the beginning,' he said, 'everything was in confusion. Then Mind came and began to create order.' Indeed, it continues to do so. The motive of all science, including space exploration, is to discover the perfection of that order.

The universe, we are told by the scientists, is running down like a clock. But who or what wound up the clock? Who or what has made a unity out of all men and their environment? Could this be the God we are looking for?

Medical science knows a great deal about the human body, thanks to long and devoted study. It still knows little about the human brain, though it does venture an opinion that on average we use only about five per cent of it. My mentor in this field of knowledge is Southend's doctor, Geoffrey Horton. Preaching in our church one Christmas Eve, he pointed out that even Einstein may have used only seven per cent of his.

When science directs the full battery of its skill towards the study of the brain and we have learned to use it all, will we then know God? Will we then know what it is that *homo sapiens* has hungered for and, instinctively, desired to worship throughout the ages?

I believe that an answer to such questions has already been given: a simple answer which appeals to my limited understanding. It was offered to us nearly 2000 years ago by the most wonderful, most knowledgeable man who ever lived on earth, with no 'ifs' or 'buts' or contorted theological argument. In the New Testament, through his disciple John, he said, plainly and straightforwardly, 'God is love.'

Was Christ divine? Of course he was. He died to prove it. The spirit within him, the spirit of the godhead so much more pure and powerful than the same spirit within us, lives on. It speaks to us, pleads with us: 'Love one another.' In this context narrow, niggling arguments concerning the physical circumstances of his birth and death are as irrelevant as arguments concerning the precise dates of Christmas and

Easter. I believe that Christ revealed God to us, in visible form. Christ was love, incarnate.

Christ asked his disciples to build a Church which would bring people together: a Church which, by example and exhortation, would establish a way of life founded upon love. 'Give to the stranger house and hospitality,' said St Columba. 'Because often, often, often goes the Christ in the stranger's guise.' Such a way of life would result in universal peace and happiness, always the desire of 'ordinary, plain folk' since, in the distant past, they began to hear in their heads a still, small voice.

(How that still, small voice came to be implanted in our brains is, as yet, a mystery. But one day, when we have learnt to use at full capacity the thousand million cells of which, at birth, each human brain is constituted, we shall know.)

Man, however, is born with instincts other than the instinct to worship a caring God. Love is suborned by hate, nobility by treachery, self-sacrifice by selfishness, innocence by hypocrisy. The Church, being man-made, finds that its spiritual content is continually being attacked by material influences, as I have tried to show, specifically, in the history of my Kirk.

> To make a happy fireside clime
>   To weans and wife,
> That's the true pathos and sublime
>   Of human life.

Robert Burns knew that love can grow best in families and in small communities. If allowed to flourish it spreads upward and outward to sweeten the whole climate of government in both Church and State. It is when this truth appears to be forgotten by the rulers and the priestly scholars, seeking temporal power for themselves and imposing their ideas upon those whom they imagine are of 'weaker capacity', that trouble comes.

The Church requires leadership and organization just as ordinary families and communities, for their own benefit, require a certain amount of State supervision. But the power base of my Kirk in Scotland, as in the early days when St Paul wrote letters to the Corinthians, the Philippians and the Romans, and when St Columba preached to the Epidii at the

Mull of Kintyre and to a Scots colony on Iona, is now acknowledged to be the voices of ordinary people.

The Church's 'one foundation' is love: love in the hearts and minds of its members, coming together in small groups to give and to receive. It follows that the most important rocks in the Church's edifice (rocks in the sense that St Peter was a rock) are the ministers of parishes in both town and country. They are the people who, by their exercise of personal love and care, can do most to show how real happiness and peace are never the result of material gain but always that of the giving and receiving of love.

It follows again that the main aim of a structured Church – in Scotland as elsewhere – should always be to uphold and strengthen the parish ministry. Sometime I think that the rulers and the priestly scholars, immersed in matters of 'policy' and in arguments concerning theology and ecumenism, are inclined to forget this. And to forget also that the credibility of the Church in Scotland reached its lowest ebb in the Middle Ages, when all the wealth and glory were seized by the mighty and the welfare and training of the humble parish priest were neglected.

About the Church today there is little of the forbidding bleakness which once distorted its image for many who sought from it love and reassurance. The dark sunglasses assumed by the 'unco pious' after the Reformation are being removed.

When my brothers and I were boys, trudging dutifully but somewhat unwillingly to church on a Sunday morning, we used to wonder about the Presbyterian forms of worship which, only seventy years ago, still retained an aura of 'black holiness'. On the one hand we sang hymns which told us to 'let all with heart and voice before His throne rejoice'. On the other hand people came to church and sat in their pews with sombre clothes and grave faces as if they considered joy a mortal sin. We suspected that it all had something to do with mourning for the death of Christ. But if Christ died to make us happy, as 'holy' people kept telling us, why was everybody so gloomy about it? Apart from anything else, was it fair to Christ?

I believe that my Kirk, as an institution, has now a brighter, happier image. It no longer emphasizes the awful punishments that await sinners. Rather does it proclaim a message of redemption and brotherhood, through love. Its tolerance is wide. It questions the arrogant claim of St Augustine that 'no salvation exists outside the Church'. Its doors, both spiritual and material, are open to all – even to 'alcoholics, prostitutes and eejits', as one old lady in Southend once put it to me.

Once again it has come to recognize, through days and nights of 'doubt and sorrow' along the years, that Christianity is what matters, not the structure of a Church or its forms of worship. Or the erudite words of 'holiness' used by orthodox theologians which tend to confuse and repel a layman's questing mind. It has studied history and identified the errors which have caused its essential purpose, the dissemination of love, to have been sullied at times by the blood and tears resulting from human selfishness and greed.

When the rulers and the priestly scholars, accepting education both divine and secular, began to offer such education to the people and then to listen to the people, the Christian cause was advanced.

Was it not the people, eagerly accepting St Columba's belief that Christian love and fellowship should influence every aspect of their workaday lives, who encouraged him to build a worldly kingdom on the foundation of a spiritual one?

Was it not the people, longing for freedom in thought and action, who forced the bishops to write the Arbroath Declaration, which declared that if the great Bruce did not please them then they would choose another king?

Was it not the people, groaning under dictatorships both royal and ecclesiastical, who produced as their champion John Knox and achieved Reformation?

Was it not the people, sick of 'revolutions', bloodshed and bitter controversies, who brought about Union in the Church of Scotland and the freedom it now enjoys?

Power based on material values will always react violently to any spiritual threat to its ascendancy. For such a power compassionate love is a dangerous concept, and Hitler and his like have dealt out death to millions in efforts to oppose it. But the Church now recognizes that the instinctive desires of the human spirit, lamely expressed and tainted with worldliness though they may be, are impossible to quell. It recognizes, too, that Christianity and politics, like God and Man, can never be separated.

(Party politics is a different question, though there are some minds too mean and limited in scope to understand this. The Bishop of Durham's Christianity was condemned as suspect by some who disliked his criticism of their party's behaviour. The Church of Scotland's Woman's Guild and the Scottish Women's Rural Institute were called 'Marxist organizations' by a Scottish MP because they appeared to disagree with one small item in his party's policy.)

When brotherly love, so often the strength of families and small communities (and of the Church), is considered by a State to be of less value than material gain, a weakness occurs which tends to create envy and division and, in the end, violence. Proof of this may be found in every blood-spattered page of my Kirk's history.

Even in this so-called age of enlightenment, when the brotherhood of man has become a trendy philosophy, what do we find? Some Protestants and Roman Catholics declaring themselves brothers in Christ but in certain circumstances murdering each other in cold blood. Some Tories and socialists – and some members of other political parties – all calling for a united people but using every weapon of propaganda to denigrate one another. Some trade unionists making great play with the word 'brotherhood' but seldom applying it to members of the CBI – or even to members of other unions. Some members of the CBI waxing holy about their brothers on the shop floor but at the end of the day still leaving some brothers more equal than others. Do they know love? Do they recognize God?

I am a member of the Church of Scotland. I love my democratic Kirk.

Because I am a Scot, with all the independence and couthiness of a Scot, I like its form of worship. But I have no quarrel with Christians who prefer forms that are different. People are different. Some find love and comfort in being told what to do. Most Scots find love and comfort in being allowed to think things out for themselves. If Christian love is there, what does it matter if worship takes place in a coloured cathedral or in a little grey kirk in a Highland glen? Or even on a 'green hill far away'?

(It seems to me that much of the strenuous work being done in the cause of ecumenism is largely wasted and might be better directed towards the universal proclamation of Christianity: simple Christianity uncluttered by ecclesiastical arguments. One day ecumenism will come. It will not be imposed from above. It will come, 'like the sun at morning', through the will of the people.)

My Kirk offers me the chance to offer and receive love. Not long ago I was in hospital, jaundiced in both body and spirit. With patient skill the doctor and nurses cured my bodily ills. But what restored positive happiness was a 'get well' letter written by the Sunday School children to their old elder, signed by themselves and underscored with dozens of X's.

One night during World War II, on a riverbank not far from Catania in Sicily, I lay shivering with fever under a groundsheet. That afternoon I had learned that my brother, an officer with the Argylls on our left flank, had been killed in action on the plain of Gerbini. There was darkness in my mind. But some light also. Even though I could not help them, I knew that my parents would be supported by the sympathetic actions of the congregation at home. And I knew that my Kirk would be with me, too.

Here in Southend, where adult membership of the Church is more than half of the population, a Christmas party is held for the old folk. It is sponsored by the local Community Council and organized by younger people in the parish. Billy Nelson, the minister, and his wife Joan are among the guests, though they are not old-age pensioners. The food is delicious, the music is bright, the stage shows are hilarious and the dancing — especially the minister's — is 'out of this world'. At the beginning we say grace before meat; at the end we sing carols. Church and State, old and young are happy together.

I believe St Columba would have enjoyed our party, even though, as he danced an eightsome reel with our hostess Fiona, his halo might slip sideways more precariously th⁻ ever.

I believe John R. Gray would have enjoyed it, too. But

he, I wonder, approve of this book and my simplistic method of showing why, in spite of its capers (and mine), I find hope and happiness in the Church of Scotland? Would he agree that Man's future depends upon the divinity within each one of us: which is God, which is Love?

Index

Bestselling Non-Fiction

☐ The Alexander Principle	Wilfred Barlow	£2.95
☐ The Complete Book of Exercises	Diagram Group	£4.95
☐ Everything is Negotiable	Gavin Kennedy	£3.50
☐ Health on Your Plate	Janet Pleshette	£4.95
☐ The Cheiro Book of Fate and Fortune	Cheiro	£2.95
☐ The Handbook of Chinese Horoscopes	Theodora Lau	£2.95
☐ Hollywood Babylon	Kenneth Anger	£7.95
☐ Hollywood Babylon II	Kenneth Anger	£7.95
☐ The Domesday Heritage	Ed. Elizabeth Hallam	£3.95
☐ Staying Off the Beaten Track	Elizabeth Gundrey	£4.95
☐ Historic Railway Disasters	O.S. Nock	£2.95
☐ Wildlife of the Domestic Cat	Roger Tabor	£4.50
☐ Elvis and Me	Priscilla Presley	£2.95
☐ Maria Callas	Arianna Stassinopoulos	£4.95
☐ The Brendan Voyage	Tim Severin	£3.95

Prices and other details are liable to change

ARROW BOOKS, BOOKSERVICE BY POST, PO BOX 29, DOUGLAS, ISLE OF MAN, BRITISH ISLES

NAME ....

ADDRESS ....

....

....

Please enclose a cheque or postal order made out to Arrow Books Ltd. for the amount due and allow the following for postage and packing.

U.K. CUSTOMERS: Please allow 22p per book to a maximum of £3.00.

B.F.P.O. & EIRE: Please allow 22p per book to a maximum of £3.00.

OVERSEAS CUSTOMERS: Please allow 22p per book.

Whilst every effort is made to keep prices low it is sometimes necessary to increase cover prices at short notice. Arrow Books reserve the right to show new retail prices on covers which may differ from those previously advertised in the text or elsewhere.

Bestselling Humour

☐ Picking on Men Again	Judy Allen & Dyan Sheldon	£1.95
☐ Carrott Roots	Jasper Carrott	£3.50
☐ A Little Zit on the Side	Jasper Carrott	£1.95
☐ The Corporate Infighter's Handbook	William Davis	£2.50
☐ The Art of Course Drinking	Michael Green	£1.95
☐ You Can See the Angel's Bum, Miss Worswick!	Mike Harding	£1.95
☐ Sex Tips for Girls	Cynthia Heimel	£2.95
☐ Sex Tips for Boys	William Davis	£2.50
☐ Lower Than Vermin	Kevin Killane	£4.95
☐ More Tales from the Mess	Miles Noonan	£2.25
☐ Limericks	Michael Palin	£1.50
☐ Dieter's Guide to Weight Loss During Sex	Richard Smith	£1.95
☐ Tales from a Long Room	Peter Tinniswood	£2.75
☐ How to Stay Topp	Simon Brett	£2.50
☐ Toyboys are More Fun	Lynne Mullen	£2.95
☐ 500 Mile Walkies	Mark Wallington	£2.50

Prices and other details are liable to change

ARROW BOOKS, BOOKSERVICE BY POST, PO BOX 29, DOUGLAS, ISLE OF MAN, BRITISH ISLES

NAME ....

ADDRESS ....

....

....

Please enclose a cheque or postal order made out to Arrow Books Ltd. for the amount due and allow the following for postage and packing.

U.K. CUSTOMERS: Please allow 22p per book to a maximum of £3.00.

B.F.P.O. & EIRE: Please allow 22p per book to a maximum of £3.00.

OVERSEAS CUSTOMERS: Please allow 22p per book.

Whilst every effort is made to keep prices low it is sometimes necessary to increase cover prices at short notice. Arrow Books reserve the right to show new retail prices on covers which may differ from those previously advertised in the text or elsewhere.

Bestselling Fiction

☐ Toll for the Brave	Jack Higgins	£2.25
☐ Basikasingo	John Matthews	£2.95
☐ Where No Man Cries	Emma Blair	£2.50
☐ Saudi	Laurie Devine	£2.95
☐ The Clogger's Child	Marie Joseph	£2.50
☐ The Gooding Girl	Pamela Oldfield	£2.95
☐ The Running Years	Claire Rayner	£2.75
☐ Duncton Wood	William Horwood	£3.50
☐ Aztec	Gary Jennings	£3.95
☐ Colours Aloft	Alexander Kent	£2.95
☐ The Volunteers	Douglas Reeman	£2.75
☐ The Second Lady	Irving Wallace	£2.95
☐ The Assassin	Evelyn Anthony	£2.50
☐ The Pride	Judith Saxton	£2.50
☐ The Lilac Bus	Maeve Binchy	£2.50
☐ Fire in Heaven	Malcolm Bosse	£3.50

Prices and other details are liable to change

ARROW BOOKS, BOOKSERVICE BY POST, PO BOX 29, DOUGLAS, ISLE OF MAN, BRITISH ISLES

NAME ....

ADDRESS ....

....

....

Please enclose a cheque or postal order made out to Arrow Books Ltd. for the amount due and allow the following for postage and packing.

U.K. CUSTOMERS: Please allow 22p per book to a maximum of £3.00.

B.F.P.O. & EIRE: Please allow 22p per book to a maximum of £3.00.

OVERSEAS CUSTOMERS: Please allow 22p per book.

Whilst every effort is made to keep prices low it is sometimes necessary to increase cover prices at short notice. Arrow Books reserve the right to show new retail prices on covers which may differ from those previously advertised in the text or elsewhere.

A Selection of Arrow Bestsellers

Prices and other details are liable to change

ARROW BOOKS, BOOKSERVICE BY POST, PO BOX 29, DOUGLAS, ISLE OF MAN, BRITISH ISLES

NAME ....

ADDRESS ....

....

....

Please enclose a cheque or postal order made out to Arrow Books Ltd. for the amount due and allow the following for postage and packing.

U.K. CUSTOMERS: Please allow 22p per book to a maximum of £3.00.

B.F.P.O. & EIRE: Please allow 22p per book to a maximum of £3.00.

OVERSEAS CUSTOMERS: Please allow 22p per book.

Whilst every effort is made to keep prices low it is sometimes necessary to increase cover prices at short notice. Arrow Books reserve the right to show new retail prices on covers which may differ from those previously advertised in the text or elsewhere.